EPHESIANS

◆

EPHESIANS

◆

H. A. IRONSIDE

Revised Edition

Introductory Notes by
Arno C. Gaebelein

LOIZEAUX
Neptune, New Jersey

First Edition, *In the Heavenlies*, 1937
Revised Edition, *Ephesians*, 2000
© 2000 by Loizeaux Brothers, Inc.

A Publication of Loizeaux Brothers, Inc.
*A Nonprofit Organization Devoted to the Lord's Work and
to the Spread of His Truth*

Unless otherwise indicated, Scripture quotations are taken from the
King James version of the Bible.

Introductory Notes taken from
Gaebelein's Concise Commentary on the Whole Bible
© 1970, 1985 by Loizeaux Brothers, Inc.

Library of Congress Cataloging-in-Publication Data

Ironside, H. A. (Henry Allan), 1876-1951.
  Ephesians / H. A. Ironside: introductory notes by Arno C. Gaebelein.—
    Rev. ed.
    p. cm.
  Rev. ed. of: In the heavenlies.
  ISBN 0-87213-432-6 (pbk.: alk. paper)
    1. Bible. N. T. Ephesians Commentaries.   I. Gaebelein, Arno
    Clemens, 1861-1945
  II. Ironside, H. A. (Henry Allan), 1876-1951. In the heavenlies.
  III. Title

BS2695.3.I76 2000
227'.507—dc21   99-25233

Printed in the United States of America
10 9 8 7 6 5 4 3 2 1

CONTENTS

Introductory Notes by Arno C. Gaebelein   7

Outline   9

Author's Introduction   11

    Ephesians 1   13

    Ephesians 2   63

    Ephesians 3   89

    Ephesians 4   101

    Ephesians 5   137

    Ephesians 6   165

Author Biography   193

INTRODUCTORY NOTES

BY ARNO C. GAEBELEIN

The Destination of the Epistle

The city of Ephesus was a place of considerable commerce and the center of the worship of the goddess Artemis (called Diana in Acts 19:24-29). Her magnificent temple was one of the wonders of the ancient world.

From Acts 18:19-21 we learn of Paul's first brief visit to that city. He was then hastening to Jerusalem to be there at Pentecost. After his visit to Jerusalem he returned to Ephesus (Acts 19:1) and labored there for about three years, so that later he could say to the elders of Ephesus, "Remember, that by the space of three years I ceased not to warn every one night and day with tears" (Acts 20:31). During this time the Ephesian assembly was founded, being composed of Jews and Gentiles who heard and believed the gospel. On his last journey to Jerusalem Paul did not visit Ephesus, but called the elders of the church to meet him at Miletus, where he said farewell and earnestly exhorted them (Acts 20:18-38).

The Epistle to the Ephesians was written by the apostle Paul while he was a prisoner. It was carried from Rome to Ephesus by Tychicus about A.D. 62 and may have been used as a kind of circular letter, being sent to and read by other assemblies as well.

The Message of the Epistle

The highest and most glorious revelation that God has been pleased to give, He has given through the apostle Paul; and his

7

Ephesian Epistle holds the place of pre-eminence. The revelation that is given in this Epistle concerning believing sinners, whom God has redeemed by the blood of His Son and exalted in Him to the highest possible position, is by far the greatest revelation. Here God is revealing His own loving heart and telling out by His Spirit how He loved us and thought of us "before the foundation of the world" (1:4). He is showing forth "the riches of his grace" (1:7) and making known the secret He held back in former ages. How rich it all is! Like God Himself, this revelation coming from His loving heart is inexhaustible.

We may speak of Ephesians as the rich Epistle of "the God and Father of our Lord Jesus Christ," who, being "rich in mercy," tells us of "the exceeding riches of his grace in his kindness toward us through Christ Jesus" (1:3; 2:4,7). But even this definition does not tell out half of all the glory this wonderful document contains. It is God's highest and God's best.

In the Psalms we read, "The heavens declare the glory of God; and the firmament sheweth his handywork" (19:1). We lift up our eyes and behold the wonders of God's creation, which He called into existence by His Son and for Him (see Colossians 1:16). In the Epistle to the Ephesians another heaven is opened. If the heavens of creation are so wonderful and their depths unfathomable, how much more wonderful are the heavenlies into which Christ has entered to be seated far above all principality and power and might, and into which God's grace has brought us in Christ!

Therefore Paul pleaded, "Walk worthy of the vocation wherewith ye are called" (4:1). What the calling is, is revealed in the first three chapters of Ephesians; and the last three chapters contain exhortations and instructions to "walk worthy" of this high calling in order to display the great masterwork of God, which is the redemption of sinners.

God's creation and His revelation, the Bible, may be studied by the telescope and the microscope. A telescopic sweep of this wonderful Epistle is hardly sufficient; it is the microscopic examination that brings out its wonders. The more we read and study this Epistle, the more we will be impressed with the greatness and the glory of the revelation it brings to our hearts. It is a theme for eternity.

OUTLINE
OF THE BOOK OF EPHESIANS

I. THE PRECIOUS DOCTRINES OF CHRIST (1:1–3:21)
   A. Our Inheritance (1:1-23)
      1. The Christian's Calling (1:1-3)
      2. Election and Predestination (1:4-5)
      3. Accepted in the Beloved (1:6)
      4. Redemption by His Blood (1:7)
      5. Gathered into One (1:8-12)
      6. Sealed with the Holy Spirit (1:13-14)
      7. Paul's Prayer for the Saints (1:15-23)
   B. Our Peace (2:1-22)
      1. The Christian's Past, Present, and Future (2:1-7)
      2. God's Workmanship (2:8-10)
      3. Made Nigh by the Blood of Christ (2:11-18)
      4. Built Together for a Habitation of God (2:19-22)
   C. Our Confidence (3:1-21)
      1. The Revelation of the Mystery (3:1-13)
      2. The Love of Christ (3:14-21)

II. THE PRACTICAL DUTIES OF CHRISTIANS (4:1–6:24)
   A. Be No More Children (4:1-32)
      1. Walking Worthy of Our Calling (4:1-6)
      2. Gifts from the Ascended Christ (4:7-13)
      3. Manifesting the Truth in Love (4:14-16)
      4. Put On the New Man (4:17-24)
      5. Grieve Not the Holy Spirit (4:25-32)
   B. Be Followers of God (5:1-33)
      1. Purity of Life (5:1-7)
      2. The Fruit of the Spirit (5:8-14)

3. The Filling of the Spirit (5:15-21)
4. The Christian Family (5:22-33)
C. Be Strong in the Lord (6:1-24)
1. The Christian Household (6:1-9)
2. The Christian's Conflict (6:10-12)
3. The Whole Armor of God (6:13-17)
4. Prayer in the Spirit (6:18-24)

AUTHOR'S
INTRODUCTION

There is nothing redundant in God's Word. Men write books and very frequently pad them in order to give quantity as well as quality, but there is nothing like that in the Bible. God's words are tried—"as silver tried in a furnace of earth, purified seven times"—and therefore we may well give our most careful attention to every item and every expression used.

What is the outstanding theme of the Epistle to the Ephesians? It opens up the truth of the privileges and responsibilities of the church as the body and bride of Christ. It brings before us our position as believers who have been quickened, raised, and seated in Christ in heavenly places.

There are very remarkable similarities between certain Old Testament books and New Testament Epistles. The Epistle to the Romans, for instance, corresponds to the book of Exodus; the letter to the Hebrews is the counterpart of Leviticus; and the Epistle to the Ephesians is the New Testament book of Joshua. In Joshua we have the people of Israel entering the possession of their inheritance. In Ephesians believers are called to enter now by faith into the possession of that inheritance which eventually we shall enjoy in all its fullness. We are far richer than we realize. All things are ours, and yet how little we appropriate!

It is said in the prophecy of Obadiah that when the Lord returns and His kingdom is established, the people of Israel shall "possess their possessions." This is a challenge to us. Do you possess your possessions? Or are your heavenly estates like castles in Spain about which you dream, but never really possess? I trust the Spirit of God may lead us into the present enjoyment of our inheritance in Christ.

For our purpose the Epistle may be divided very simply, without breaking it up into many portions that would be difficult to carry in our memories. We shall divide it into two parts, the first three chapters giving us the doctrine, and the last three, the practical outcome; the first division gives us our inheritance, and the last, the behavior that should characterize those who are so richly blessed. Often that is the divine order of Scripture: instruction in the truth first, practice in accordance with the truth afterwards.

EPHESIANS 1

The Sphere of Christian Privilege (1:1-3)

As we look at the opening verse of Ephesians we are struck at
once by the name of the writer, Paul. Thirteen New Testament
Epistles begin with the word *Paul*. Another one is undoubtedly from
Paul, but begins with the magnificent word *God*. I refer to the Epistle
to the Hebrews. Do we stop to inquire as often as we should how
this man ever came to be called Paul? That was not his name origi-
nally. His name in the first place was Saul. He was a Benjamite, and
bore the name of the first king of Israel, who came from the tribe of
Benjamin. For many years Paul was a haughty, self-righteous Pharisee, proud of his genealogy and his religious zeal, until one day he
had a meeting with our Lord Jesus Christ. Have you had such a
meeting? From that moment on everything was changed for him.
He could say:

> I was journeying in the noon-tide,
> When His light shone o'er my road;
> And I saw Him in the glory,
> Saw Him, Jesus, Son of God.
>
> Marvel not that Christ in glory
> All my inmost soul hath won;
> I have seen a light from heaven,
> Far beyond the brightest sun.

13

That vision of Christ changed Saul the Pharisee, into Paul, the humble servant of Christ. He did not use his new name immediately, you remember. It seems to have been taken after he won his first outstanding Gentile convert, Sergius Paulus, in the Isle of Cyprus. It appears to have been given him in recognition of his apostolic ministry. It means "the little one," a wonderful name for one who once thought himself so great; but that is what Christ does for one. As Paul wrote

> What things were gain to me, those I counted loss for Christ. Yea doubtless, and I count all things but loss for the excellency of the knowledge of Christ Jesus my Lord: for whom I have suffered the loss of all things, and do count them but dung, that I may win Christ (Philippians 3:7-8).

All that Saul gloried in, Paul flung away for Jesus' sake. He was content to be little, "less than the least of all saints," that in him Christ Jesus might exhibit His boundless patience.

I remember going to a camp meeting, and the dear folk were singing a little chorus that went like this:

> The quickest way up is down,
> The quickest way up is down;
> You may climb up high, and try and try,
> But the quickest way up is down.

How long it takes some of us to learn that lesson! We are always trying to become somebody, and forgetting that Jesus said, "Whosoever will save his life shall lose it: and whosoever will lose his life, for my sake shall find it" (Matthew 16:25). Blessed is the princely Saul when he becomes the little Paul, bowing at the Savior's feet.

Paul called himself an apostle. Just what is an *apostle*? The word might be translated "a messenger," "a sent one," "one sent on a mission," and so there is a certain sense in which every missionary is an apostle. But there is a higher sense in which the word *apostle* refers to those who were specially commissioned by our Lord Jesus

Christ to go out to the world and carry the truth through which the church was instituted. Paul was not among those who knew the Lord on earth, but he was ordained an apostle to the nations by His personal appointment when the risen Christ appeared to him that day on the Damascus road. He said to him, "I have appeared unto thee for this purpose, to make thee a minister and a witness both of these things which thou hast seen, and of those things in the which I will appear unto thee" (Acts 26:16). And so Paul, the apostle of Jesus Christ by the will of God, could go forth saying:

> Christ the Son of God hath sent me
> Through the midnight lands;
> Mine the mighty ordination
> Of the pierced hands.

I do not like to touch on critical questions in these studies, and yet I must do so here. Some people do not notice divine names carefully, and this is the reason why those who copied the manuscripts were not always particular whether they wrote "Jesus Christ," or "Christ Jesus." Peter, James, John, and Jude spoke of our Lord as "Jesus Christ." But in Ephesians 1:1 Paul spoke of "Christ Jesus." Why? Because *Jesus* is His human name and in resurrection He was made Lord and *Christ*. The disciples knew Him on earth as Jesus, the self-humbled One. But Paul never knew Him in that way; he never knew Him as Jesus on earth. He had his first sight of Him in the glory, and his soul was so thrilled with what he saw that he never thought of Him as other than the glorified One. So he invariably wrote in the original text, "Christ Jesus," and his message is in a peculiar sense called "The gospel of the glory." The other disciples walked with Him on earth and delighted to remember Him as He was when here, and so they spoke of Him as "Jesus Christ." Any critical version will make this distinction clear.

Paul was a messenger, a sent one of Christ Jesus "by the will of God." It was no mere idle thought of his that sent him on this mission. It was not that he concluded it would be the best way to spend his life. He who saved him commissioned him, and sent him forth to be a teacher of the Gentiles in faith and truth. So he insisted on the divine character of his commission, "An apostle of Christ Jesus by the will of God."

A simple cobbler was being introduced to a rather dignified clergyman, and when the cobbler said, "I didn't get your name," the clergyman replied, "The Reverend Doctor Blank, by the will of God." The cobbler said, "And I am John Doe, cobbler by the will of God. I am glad to meet you, sir." It is a great thing, whatever your station in life may be, to recognize it as "by the will of God." Am I a preacher of the gospel? It should be only because I have heard a divine call urging me and thrusting me out. Am I a merchant? Have I been called to make money for the glory of God? Then let me remember that I am a merchant by the will of God. I should be sure that I am where God's will has placed me, and should seek to be faithful to Him.

The apostle addressed himself, "To the saints which are at Ephesus, and to the faithful in Christ Jesus." One might suppose that he was addressing two classes of people: *saints*, that is all believers, and *the faithful*, that is a spiritual aristocracy. However, this verse might better be rendered, "To the saints which are at Ephesus, even the believers in Christ Jesus." In other words, it is faith in Christ Jesus that designates a person a saint. Are you a saint? You say, "I wouldn't like to go so far. I am not sinless yet." A saint is not a sinless person; a saint is a separated person, separated to God in Christ Jesus. People have an idea that if you live a very saintly life, eventually you may become a saint. God says, "Do you believe in My Son? Have you trusted Him? Very well, then, I constitute you a saint; be sure that you live in a saintly way." We do not become saints by saintliness, but we should be characterized by saintliness because we are saints.

In verse 2 we have the apostolic salutation, "Grace be to you, and peace, from God our Father, and from the Lord Jesus Christ." He is not referring at all to saving grace. These people were already saved. He tells them, "By grace are ye saved through faith; and that not of yourselves: it is the gift of God: Not of works, lest any man should boast" (Ephesians 2:8-9). It is a great thing to have your salvation settled.

The lack of positive conviction and definite assurance comes out

in a great many of the hymns we sing. How hard it is to find hymns
that are absolutely Scriptural. In a meeting some time ago I was
giving a message on "The Indwelling Holy Spirit." At the close of
the service, the dear pastor stood up and said, "In the light of this
splendid address, let us sing, 'Holy Spirit, faithful Guide, ever near
the Christian's side.'" I felt my heart sink as I thought, *After I have
spent forty minutes trying to show them that the Holy Spirit is not
merely at our side, but dwells in us, they haven't got it yet.* Then
they came to that last gloomy verse, and I said, "Please don't sing
that verse":

> When our days of toil shall cease,
> Waiting still for sweet release;
> Nothing left but heaven and prayer,
> Wond'ring if our names are there;
> Wading deep the dismal flood,
> Pleading naught but Jesus' blood.

What a mixture! I refuse to sing it. I *know* my name is there! I do
not understand how it is that Christians are so slow in laying hold of
divine truth.

Here in Ephesians 1:2 the apostle means grace to keep and preserve us, not grace to save. For the believer, salvation is already
settled for eternity, but we need daily grace for daily trials.

How does one obtain this grace?

> We have not an high priest which cannot be touched with the
> feeling of our infirmities; but was in all points tempted like as
> we are, yet without sin. Let us therefore come boldly unto the
> throne of grace, that we may obtain mercy, and find grace to
> help in time of need (Hebrews 4:15-16).

We were saved by grace, we began with grace, but we need grace
every step of the way that we might triumph over the world and
over the natural propensities of our poor hearts. As Christians we
have the nature of the old man in us still, and it will readily manifest
itself if not subdued and kept in place by grace divine.

"Grace be to you, and peace." This is not peace *with* God, which was made for us by the blood of Calvary's cross. Every believer in the Lord Jesus should know what it is to "have peace with God through our Lord Jesus Christ" (Romans 5:1). But this is the peace *of* God, occupying and protecting our hearts as we move along toward our heavenly home—the same peace that filled the heart of Jesus when here on earth.

May I use an illustration from the life of Jesus to illustrate this peace? In Luke 8 we read that one day Jesus said to His disciples in the ship, "Let us go over to the other side." Where were they going? To the other side of the lake. When they got into the boat, He went to sleep in perfect peace, and in the middle of the night the elements raged, the devil stirred up a terrific tempest, but it could not drown Him. It was impossible that the boat in which He sailed should founder. But the disciples were terrified and they aroused that holy sleeper and said, "Master, Master, we perish!" Jesus, wakened from His sleep, looked at them and said, "Where is your faith?" In Matthew 8:26 we read that He said to them, "Why are ye fearful, O ye of little faith?" He called them men of "little faith," with the thunder roaring, the lightning flashing, the wind blowing a gale, and the sea raging around them. You surely could not blame men for being afraid under those circumstances! But you see, Jesus had not said to them, "Let us go out into the middle of the lake and get drowned." He said, "Let us go over to the other side," and they should have rested on His word. They would have had the same peace that He had if they had believed His word.

Do the trials of life sometimes test your soul? Do you wonder what will become of you? This is what will become of you: If worst comes to worst and you starve to death, you are going home to Heaven! Thousands of people are dying and going to a lost eternity, but no matter what comes to you, if you are saved, you are going home! As we realize that we are in His hand, the peace of God, like a military garrison, keeps our hearts and saves us from all doubt and fear.

"Grace be to you, and peace, from God our Father" (Ephesians 1:2). Do you love to dwell on those words, "From God our Father"? The Lord came to reveal the Father, and the Holy Spirit enables us to know the Father, and one of the first evidences that a man is born of God is that he lifts his heart to Heaven and says "Father." This is not the doctrine of the universal fatherhood of God and brotherhood of man. That is not what the apostle was writing about. He was addressing saints, believers in Christ Jesus, and when he wrote to them, he said, "God our Father." It is only by regeneration, only by the second birth, that we enter into this blessed relationship. Scripture declares that those who have never been regenerated are of the flesh, they are not the children of God. Our Lord Jesus said to certain ones, "Ye are of your father the devil, and the lusts of your father ye will do" (John 8:44). That does not sound very much like the universal fatherhood of God and the brotherhood of man! People tell me that is what Jesus came to teach. I defy anyone to find any such thing anywhere in all the teaching of our Lord Jesus Christ. He said to Nicodemus, "Except a man be born again, he cannot see the kingdom of God" (John 3:3). In that verse He denied the universal fatherhood of God and brotherhood of man. I know all men are brothers in Adam and we are one in sin, but it is only by a new birth that one can become a brother of the saints and a child of God.

"Grace be to you, and peace, from God our Father, and from the Lord Jesus Christ." The Holy Spirit delights to give our Savior His full title, "the Lord Jesus Christ." He is Lord of all, and therefore all men are called to subject themselves to Him.

Notice Ephesians 1:3, for in this we properly begin the study of the Epistle: "Blessed be the God and Father of our Lord Jesus Christ." He has said before that God is our Father, and now points out that in a peculiar sense God sustains that relationship with the Lord Jesus Christ. He is the *God* of our Lord Jesus Christ because Jesus became man, and as man He looks up to the Father as His God. He is the *Father* of our Lord Jesus Christ because Christ is God the Son from all eternity. What a wealth of instruction is bound up in that expression, "The God and Father of our Lord Jesus Christ." It was not until the resurrection that He revealed this unique relationship. He said to Mary, "Go to my brethren, and say unto them, I ascend unto my Father, and your Father, and to my God, and your God" (John 20:17). He does not say, "I ascend to *our* God and *our* Father." His relationship is different from ours. He was not simply a man brought into union with God, but He was the Son of God, come down to earth in grace, who became man for our redemption.

Farther on in this Epistle there are two prayers—one in the last part of this chapter, and the other in chapter 3—and they agree in a very striking way with these titles. In chapter 1:17 Paul prayed that "the God of our Lord Jesus Christ" may do certain things. Then when we turn to chapter 3:14 we read, "For this cause I bow my knees unto the Father of our Lord Jesus Christ." Why the difference? Because in the first prayer he spoke of the divine counsels and power, and so he addressed himself to God. In the second prayer he considered our relationship to God and addressed himself to "the Father of our Lord Jesus Christ." Scripture is wonderfully accurate.

"Blessed be the God and Father of our Lord Jesus Christ, who hath blessed us with all spiritual blessings in heavenly places in Christ." Notice, "He *hath* blessed us." The apostle was not writing of something that may be ours when we get to Heaven, but right here and now I have been blessed with every spiritual blessing in Christ Jesus. People often ask me if I have obtained the second blessing yet, and I generally say, "Second blessing? Why, I am somewhere up in the hundreds of thousands as far as that goes, if you refer to experience. But actually I obtained *every* blessing that God has for a redeemed sinner when I put my trust in the Lord Jesus Christ." He does not just give us a little now and a little later, but gives us everything in Christ. It is all yours. Enter into it and enjoy it.

It is one thing to have the blessings and another thing to make them yours. I read about a man in Montana for whom authorities had been searching for a long time. Some years ago a British nobleman died, leaving an estate which, as he had no children, would go to the next nearest relative. This man away out west was the nearest heir, living in poverty, and just eking out a struggling existence when they found him and gave him the news that the estate was his. It was his all the time, but he did not know it. What did he do when he found it out? Did he say, "Well, it is a good thing to know that I have something to fall back on and some day I will go and look at it"? No, he went downtown, and on the strength of the good news bought himself a new suit and a ticket, and left for Great Britain. I read an interview that the reporters had with him. They asked, "Where are you going?" He answered, "To take possession of my estate." You and I are richer far than he was, but do we really take possession by faith of the things that are ours in Christ?

You may say, "But name some of these things that are ours." He has blessed us with the blessing of forgiveness of our sins, with justification from all things, with sanctification in Christ, with a robe of perfect righteousness, with a heavenly citizenship, by giving us a place in the body of Christ, and making us heirs of His riches through Christ! And yet how some of us struggle along, eking out a poor, wretched, miserable existence! We act as spiritual paupers when we ought to be living like millionaires. God has made Christ Jesus to be our wisdom, righteousness, sanctification, and redemption, and yet for six years after I was converted I was still seeking righteousness and sanctification. But one day I woke up to the fact that it was all mine in Christ Jesus, and that I had simply to appropriate and enjoy it.

Now notice that Paul wrote that my blessings are secure in Heaven, and He calls me in the Spirit to rise to my heavenly citizenship and live in this world as a heavenly man should live. I may draw from God all the resources I need to be more than conqueror day by day, as I pass through this world.

Notice how carefully you have to read Scripture: "Who hath blessed us with all spiritual blessings in heavenly places in Christ." What a mistake it would be to translate that, "with Christ." Do you see the difference? How often we hear people misquote Ephesians 2:6, and say that God has "made us sit together in heavenly places *with* Christ Jesus." Nothing of the kind. We are not seated together *with* Christ; we are seated *in* Him. He is there as our representative, and that is an altogether different thing from being seated *with* Him. This does not mean that we are only privileged and seated together in Christ when we have a real, good, happy, spiritual meeting. Sometimes when we have a good meeting and the people think they have been helped, some well-meaning brother closes in prayer and says, "O Lord, we thank Thee that we have been sitting together in heavenly places in Christ Jesus this morning." I say to myself, *The dear brother hasn't got it yet. He thinks because there is a glow in his heart, because he feels happy, that means he is sitting in heavenly places in Christ.* But I am sitting in heavenly places in Christ just as truly when I am oppressed with the trials of the way, as I am when I am flourishing and have everything that my heart could desire. It is a question of fact: Christ is in the heavenlies, and God sees me in Him. I am blessed in Him, and all the treasures of Heaven are at my disposal, and I am to draw on them as I have need in order that I may be strengthened and able to rejoice as I go forth in His service down here.

Our Election and Predestination (1:4-5)

Next the apostle carries our minds back to the past eternity that we may be brought to realize that salvation is altogether of God, not at all of ourselves. An old hymn puts it this way:

> 'Tis not that I did choose Thee,
> For, Lord, that could not be,
> This heart would still refuse Thee,
> But Thou hast chosen me.

And again in another hymn that we know well, we are taught to sing:

> Jesus sought me when a stranger,
> Wand'ring from the fold of God;
> He, to rescue me from danger,
> Interposed His precious blood.
>   Robert Robinson

It was God Himself who purposed our salvation in the past eternity. It is Jesus Christ who accomplished our salvation on the cross when the fullness of time had come. It is God the Holy Spirit who convicts us and brings us to repentance and to a saving knowledge of the grace of God as revealed in Christ. We cannot take any credit to ourselves for our salvation. A little boy was asked, "Have you found Jesus?" He looked up and said, "Please, sir, I didn't know He was lost; but I was, and He found me." We did not have to do the seeking after Him, He sought us because of the love that was in His heart from eternity.

"According as he hath chosen us in him before the foundation of the world" (Ephesians 1:4). This, of course, is the truth of election. Again and again believers are spoken of as elect people, as children chosen of God. Charles Spurgeon said, "God certainly must have chosen me before I came into this world or He never would have done so afterwards." He set His love on us in the past eternity. This troubles people sometimes, and yet how could it be otherwise? God who is infinite in wisdom, with whom the past and the future are all one eternal *now,* purposed in His heart before the world came into existence that He was going to have a people who would be to the praise and glory of His grace for all eternity. He looked down through the ages and saw us as those for whom He would give His Son in order to add to the glory of the Lord Jesus Christ. It is wonderful to see how intimately the joy of Christ and our salvation are linked together. John Bunyan said, "Oh, this Lamb of God! He had a whole heaven to Himself, myriad of angels to do His bidding, but these could not satisfy Him. He must have sinners to share it with Him."

Notice that it is God who purposes salvation this way; it is God who plans; it was God who chose us in Christ before the foundation of the world. Notice, it is not that He chose the church as such, but he chose every individual who was to be a member of that church, to be one with Christ for eternity. You say, "I do not understand that." I don't either. Whenever I consider a subject such as God's electing grace and predestinating love, I remind myself that the Word says, "My thoughts are not your thoughts, neither are your ways my ways, saith the Lord. For as the heavens are higher than the earth, so are my ways higher than your ways, and my thoughts than your thoughts" (Isaiah 55:8-9). But it may help us a little if we consider predestination apart from the question of the fall of man. Before the world was made, before sin came in, God chose us in Christ to be with His Son for all eternity. The fact that sin came in did not alter God's purpose. He is still going to carry it out in spite of all that Satan has done to wreck His fair creation.

The purpose of God is according to His grace, grace to those who could not earn it, who did not deserve anything but eternal judgment. Somebody has well said, "The truth of election is a family secret." It is not something that we go out and proclaim to the world. We read, "Cast not your pearls before swine," and swine, you know, are unclean. We are not to go to unsaved men in the uncleanness of their sin and talk about election. They would not understand it at all. It is a family secret that God loves to whisper in the ears of His beloved children.

The doctrine of election has been pictured in this way. Here is a vast host of people hurrying down the broad road with their minds fixed on their sins, and one person stands calling attention to a door—the entrance into the narrow way that leads to life eternal. On this door is plainly written the text, "Whosoever will, let him come." Every man is invited, no one need hesitate. Some may say, "Well, I may not be of the elect, and so it would be useless for me to endeavor to come, for the door will not open for me." But God's invitation is absolutely sincere: it is addressed to every man, "Whosoever will, let him take of the water of life freely" (Revelation 22:17). If men refuse to come, if they pursue their own godless way down to the pit, whom can they blame but themselves for their eternal judgment? The messenger addressed himself to all, the call comes to all, the door could be entered by all, but many refuse to come and perish in their sins. Such men can never blame God for their eternal destruction. The door was open, the invitation was given, they refused. God says to them sorrowfully, "Ye will not come unto me, that ye might have life." But as the invitation is extended, every minute or two someone stops and asks, "What is that?" "The way to life," is the reply. "Ah, that I might find the way to life! I have found no satisfaction in this old world. I should like to know how to be free from my sin, how to be made fit for the presence of God." Then he draws near and listens, and the Spirit of God impresses the message on his heart and conscience. As a result he says, "I am going inside: I will accept the invitation; I will enter that door," and he presses his way in and it shuts behind him. As he turns about he finds written on the inside of the door the words, "Chosen in Christ before the foundation of the world." "What?" he says, "had God His heart fixed on me before ever the world came into being?" Yes, but he could not find it out until he got inside. You see, you can pass the door if you will, you can trample the love of God beneath your feet, you can spurn His grace if you are determined to do it, but you will go down to the pit and you will be responsible for your own doom.

There is no such thing taught in the Word of God as predestination to eternal condemnation. If men are lost, they are lost because they do not come to Christ. When men do come to Christ, they learn the wonderful secret that God has foreknown it all from eternity, and that He had settled it before the world came into existence that they were to share the glory of His Son throughout endless ages. D. L. Moody used to say in his quaint way, when people talked about the subject of election, "the whosoever wills are the elect, and the whosoever wont's are the non-elect." And so you can settle it for yourself whether you will be among the elect of God or not.

When asked to explain the doctrine of election, a brother once said, "Well, it's this way, the Lord voted for my salvation; the devil voted for my damnation. I voted with the Lord, and so we got into the majority." The devil seeks my eternal loss and God seeks my eternal blessing, and my heart says, "I will." I then know that I am among those chosen in Christ before the foundation of the world. Let me link this up with another Scripture, 2 Thessalonians 2:13, "But we are bound to give thanks alway to God for you, brethren beloved of the Lord, because God hath from the beginning chosen you to salvation through sanctification of the Spirit and belief of the truth." There you have the purpose of God in the past eternity. God had from the beginning chosen you unto salvation, and He is carrying out His purpose through the work of the Holy Spirit as the one who hears the message believes the truth.

Then listen to the apostle Peter, "Elect according to the foreknowledge of God the Father, through sanctification of the Spirit, unto obedience and sprinkling of the blood of Jesus Christ: Grace unto you, and peace, be multiplied" (1 Peter 1:2). There you have exactly the same order. God the Father foreknew us from eternity, but it was up to us whether or not we would yield to Christ. When we did yield in the obedience of faith, we took our places beneath the sprinkled blood of Jesus and our salvation was eternally assured.

People try sometimes to put the whole responsibility on God and say, "If God has not chosen me, I cannot be saved." If you will trust in Christ, you may know that God has chosen you.

You remember the striking illustration that the Spirit of God Himself gave us at the end of the book of Acts. When Paul and his company were on their way to Rome, a terrific storm arose, and they were casting out some of the cargo in order to lighten the ship, but finally they gave up in despair. And then an angel appeared and spoke with Paul, and Paul called for the captain of the ship and said:

> I exhort you to be of good cheer: for there shall be no loss of any man's life among you, but of the ship. For there stood by me this night the angel of God, whose I am, and whom I serve, Saying, Fear not, Paul; thou must be brought before Caesar: and, lo, God hath given thee all them that sail with thee (Acts 27:22-24).

There was God's foreknowledge. Everyone in that ship would be brought through safely, not one of them would be lost. But a little while afterwards Paul noticed something going on among the sailors. They were fitting out a boat and were preparing to launch it into the sea, putting some provisions into it and getting ready to cut away and leave the ship. And Paul said to the captain, "Except these abide in the ship, ye cannot be saved" (Acts 27:31). Had he not already told them that no one would perish? That was God's side; their side was to "abide in the ship." They were responsible to see that no one left the ship, and so it is in regard to the doctrine of election and man's responsibility. Everyone who is saved will be in Heaven because he was chosen in Christ before the foundation of the world, and yet every man who is ever saved will be there because as a guilty sinner he put his personal trust in the Lord Jesus Christ. You may say, "I can't reconcile these two ideas to each other." You do not need to do so; just believe it and go on your way rejoicing.

Look at Ephesians 1:4, "According as he hath chosen us in him before the foundation of the world, that we should be holy and without blame before him." God, who foresaw all who would put their trust in Christ, provided a means whereby all our sin and iniquity could be paid for, in order that we might be presented holy and without blame before Him. This, of course, involves the work of the cross. Redemption was not an afterthought with God. It was all provided for when He decided to bring into existence creatures who could give Him voluntary love and service.

The questions may be asked, Why did not God who knows all things create a race of people who would not have sinned and rejected Him, but who would always have done that which was right in His sight, who would always have loved and obeyed Him? Is not God in some sense responsible for sin because He created a creature weak enough to sin? Could He not have created one so strong that he could not have sinned? Certainly He could. He could have made creatures that could not have failed Him. He could have created humanity in such a way that it could not have deviated from the right path. But God's determination to create a man or woman who could *choose* to give Him loyal obedience, loving service, and voluntary devotion, necessitated the creation of men and women who could turn away from God if they wanted to and refuse to obey Him if they so desired. Otherwise there would have been no freedom in their love, devotion, reverence, and affection. God was willing to take all the risk that He did take in order to have beings in this universe who would give Him glad and free-hearted love and devotion. So when sin came in, the Savior was given, and the Seed of the woman has bruised the serpent's head. Now through the work of Christ, God can present us in His glorious presence holy and without blame in Him. It is not what we are naturally in ourselves, but what we are in Christ Jesus.

Now notice in Ephesians 1:5 we have another word that troubles people. We read, "In love having predestinated us." You will notice that I began reading verse 5 with the last part of verse 4. I ended verse 4 with the word *him*——"That we should be holy and without blame before him." The King James version ends verse 4 this way: "That we should be holy and without blame before him in love." But I believe a better translation is to add the phrase, "in love," to the beginning of verse 5: "In love having predestinated us unto the adoption of children by Jesus Christ to himself, according to the good pleasure of his will." One is not so afraid of the word *predestinated* when it is preceded by the word *love*. There is no arbitrariness there, but it is all "in love." Predestination is a manifestation of the love of the Father. As it is God who chose us in grace, it is the Father who had predestinated us to the adoption of children. Nowhere in the Bible are people ever predestined to go to Hell, and nowhere are people simply predestined to go to Heaven. Look it up and see. We are chosen in Christ to share His glory for eternity, but predestination is always to some special place of blessing.

In Romans 8:29 we read: "For whom he did foreknow, he also did predestinate to be conformed to the image of his Son, that he might be the firstborn among many brethren." Predestined to what? Predestined "to be conformed to the image of his Son." You see, predestination is not God from eternity saying, "This man goes to Heaven and this man to Hell." No, but predestination teaches me that when I have believed in Christ and trusted Him as my Savior, I may know on the authority of God that it is settled forever that some day I am to become exactly like my Savior. It settles the question of the security of my salvation. Whatever my present unsatisfactory experiences may be, some day I shall be altogether like the One who has redeemed me.

"Having predestinated us unto the adoption of children by Jesus Christ to himself" (Ephesians 1:5). The word *adoption* perplexes some. They say, "Does it mean that we are only adopted children and not really born into the family? Does it mean adopted in that sense?" This word literally means, the full placing as sons. We might read this verse, "Having predestinated us unto the son-placing through Jesus Christ unto Himself." It will help us to understand this concept of adoption better if we bear in mind that in the days when our Bible was written, a man might have a number of wives and some who were really his slaves. He would have to select those children among whom he wished to divide his estate for he might not wish it divided among all his various children. He would take those whom he selected as his heirs down to the forum, and there confess them openly before the proper authority as his sons and then go through a ceremony of adoption. From that day on they were recognized as his heirs. We have been born into the family of God by regeneration and thus made children of God. We have received the Holy Spirit, who is the Spirit of adoption, and God has marked us out as those who will share everything with the Son for all eternity. We are adopted sons and born-again children.

"In love having predestinated us unto the adoption of children by Jesus Christ to himself, according to the good pleasure of his will." Our Lord is the One through whom all this blessing comes. There is a beautiful passage in the Old Testament that speaks of the coming Savior as a "nail in a sure place" (Isaiah 22:23). The simile is taken from the tent-life of the nomadic people. Pegs, on which they hung their garments and blankets, were fitted into the upright poles of their tents, and the women hung the utensils they used on similar pegs. Scripture pictures all kinds of vessels hung on one of these nails fastened in a sure place, and it says, "And they shall hang upon him all the glory of his father's house" (Isaiah 22:24). So the Lord Jesus Christ having accomplished redemption has become that "nail in a sure place," and every one of us are hung upon Him. If the nail goes down, we all go down; if Christ fails, then we all go down together. But since Christ will never fail, then He will sustain every one of us right on to the very end. That is the truth that is revealed here.

This truth of election and predestination and of sonship emphasizes the preciousness of our Lord Jesus Christ! Say it over and over to your soul until your whole being is thrilled, "Lord Jesus, I owe it all to You." Then you will begin to understand why one enraptured with His love could sing:

> Jesus, the very thought of Thee
> With sweetness fills my breast;
> But sweeter far Thy face to see,
> And in Thy presence rest.
>   Bernard of Clairvaux

Every blessing for time and eternity we owe to Him. Are those blessings given to us according to our understanding or the strength of our faith, or our devotedness? Not at all! What then? "According to the good pleasure of his will." You know some people are afraid of the will of God, yet it is the will of God that you and I who put our trust in the Lord Jesus should share the Savior's glory for all eternity. And in revealing His will to us step by step along the way, He would have us become more and more conformed to Him while here on earth. Oh, to be able to say from the heart, "I welcome Your sweet will, O God." The greatest mistake any Christian can make is to substitute his own will for the will of God.

Remember, it is the will of God that every saved one should eventually be with Christ and like Christ forevermore.

> I know not where His hand shall lead,
> Through desert wastes, or flowery mead;
> 'Mid tangled thicket set with thorn,
> 'Mid gloom of night or glow of morn;
> But still I know my Father's hand
> Will bring me to His goodly land.

If you are still unsaved, the most fearful mistake you can ever make is to suppose that if you yield yourself to the will of God it would take away from your peace and happiness and joy. The only real peace, the only real happiness, the only real joy for created beings is found in following the will of God. His will planned our redemption, His will purposed our salvation, and His will secures our place in the glory for all eternity.

Accepted in the Beloved (1:6)

You will at once recognize the fact that this verse does not in itself constitute a complete sentence. It is a part of a rather lengthy sentence that began with the third verse. We have been climbing one of God's wonderful mountain peaks from verse 3, and now we have reached the top. Standing here at verse 6, we are privileged to look below us and see the depths from which we have come, and then look beyond and see the glory that is before us.

There is no room for human boasting. Our salvation is according to the good pleasure of God's will, to the praise of the glory of His own grace, and no man may give himself any credit whatsoever. It is to the praise of the glory of God's grace that He has accepted us in the Beloved. I hope we are all clear about grace. We are constantly preaching about it, singing about it, and reading about it, and yet how few there are who really understand the precious fact that our salvation is altogether of grace. No matter how many times one may preach on salvation by grace, every time he rises to face an audience there are many who are still strangers to the grace of God. Let us never forget that grace is God's free unmerited favor lavished on those who deserve nothing but His judgment. You cannot earn grace, you cannot earn His lovingkindness.

You may remember the case of the woman who attempted the assassination of Queen Elizabeth I. She was dressed as a page, and had hid herself in the queen's boudoir awaiting the convenient moment to stab her to death, not realizing that the queen's attendants would be very careful to search the rooms before her majesty was permitted to retire. Hidden there among the gowns they found this woman and brought her into the presence of the queen. They took from her the dagger that she had hoped to plant in the heart of her sovereign. She realized that her case, humanly speaking, was hopeless, and so she threw herself down on her knees and pleaded and begged the queen to have compassion on her and show her grace. Queen Elizabeth looked at her quietly, and coolly said, "If I show you grace, what promise will you make for the future?" The woman looked up and said, "Grace that hath conditions, grace that is fettered by precautions, is no grace at all." Queen Elizabeth understood immediately and said, "You are right; I pardon you of my grace," and they led her away a free woman. History tells us that from that moment Queen Elizabeth had no more faithful devoted servant than that woman who had intended to take her life.

Remember, grace that has conditions, grace that is bound by precautions, that insists on pledges and promises for the future, is no grace at all. Grace is favor freely shown to those who deserve only judgment, and so we read that our salvation is to the praise of the glory of His grace. When at last we get home to Heaven, He will have all the praise and all the glory. We will gratefully acknowledge in His glorious presence that left to ourselves we would have gone on to everlasting judgment, that it was He who showed us our deep, deep need. Looking down on us He pitied us as we were hurrying on to endless woe and He gave His Son to die. This is the grace of our Lord Jesus that led Him to go to Calvary's cross and settle the claim that we never could have settled. And so by grace, and by grace alone, have we been saved.

Observe that we have been made "accepted in the beloved." The saved sinner does not stand before God in any righteousness of his own, nor does he plead any merit of his own before the divine throne. Not merely forgiven, not merely justified, not merely washed from his sins or cleansed from his defilement, he is received in lovingkindness to the very heart of God according to the Father's estimate of His own beloved Son. In John 17 we read our Lord's prayer to the Father for His own—you and me, if we have believed in Him, for He was praying for those "who shall believe on me through their word." Thus He included all believers to the very end of time, and speaking of such He said to the Father, "That the world may know that thou...hast loved them, as thou hast loved me." I could not believe that statement if it were not in my Bible. I could not believe that God the holy One loves me, a poor sinner in myself, as He loves the Lord Jesus Christ, His spotless Son.

We do not have far to go for the proof of His love. It is seen in that God commended His love toward us by sending His Son to be the propitiation for our sins. If He gave His Son for me, then He must love me as greatly as He loves His Son, or He never would have permitted Him to die for me. Also in 1 John 4:17 we read a similar passage: "That we may have boldness in the day of judgment: because as he is, so are we in this world," that is, as He is in relation to judgment. He has already passed through the judgment and will never have to go into it again. He will never again know the forsaking of God, the enshrouding of His soul with the blackness of darkness, the taste of the bitter cup, the agony, shame, and curse of the cross. All that is in the past. He went through it all for us and now so truly are we linked up with Him that "as he is, so are we in this world."

A very interesting volume was published, giving the story of the life and work of Dr. Usher, who for a great many years carried on medical missionary work in Turkey. In this wonderful story he related an incident that illustrates in a striking way what we have before us. He told how a notable member of the Turkish movement had become governor of a certain province in which the mission hospital and schools were located. This man was very learned and of great determination, but a very rigid Muslim. He had made up his mind to carry out one of the old laws of Turkey stating that foreigners coming into the country should be allowed to live there for one year, but if at the end of that time they had not become Mohammedans, they would have to leave Turkey. That law had been a dead issue for a great many years, but he made up his mind that he would banish all the missionaries, Catholic and Protestant, from his province.

However, he decided that to be fair he would give them all an opportunity to become Mohammedans, and so during the month of Ramadan, their annual fast, he invited all these missionaries to a great feast in his home. They were allowed to feast at night but not in the daytime. As all these missionaries received the message, they knew it to be a summons. According to Turkish law it would never do to make excuses, for the invitation to dine with the governor was tantamount to a command. Dr. Usher sat on the left hand of the governor, and the Catholic bishop sat on his right hand, with the other missionaries on either side, and a number of the attendants of the governor in waiting.

After a while turning to the Catholic bishop, the governor said, "My lord bishop, will you tell me how you think a man can enter paradise?" The bishop answered, "I will say that I believe through the merits of Jesus Christ, God can forgive my sins and take me to paradise." "Not at all," said the governor; "I cannot believe that God is less righteous than I am, and I do not believe it would be righteous for God because of His friendship for another, to forgive a sinner and take him to paradise. If someone here had become in-debted to the government and I had to put him in prison, and some-one said, 'That man is a friend of mine, for my sake I beg you let him go free,' no matter how much I would desire to please my friend, I would be an unrighteous governor to let him go free simply be-cause of my friendship for someone who was interested in him. I do not believe that God is less righteous than I." The bishop had not another word to say and sat there looking puzzled.

Dr. Usher felt that something tremendous was at stake, and he knew that he would be questioned next, so he lifted his heart to God, remembering the verse, "When they deliver you up, take no thought how or what ye shall speak: for it shall be given you in that same hour what ye shall speak" (Matthew 10:19). He prayed, "Lord, by Thy Spirit give me now the message."

The governor turned and said, "What would you say? How may a man be assured of an entrance into paradise?" Dr. Usher replied, "Your Excellency, will you permit me to use your own illustration, only to change it slightly? Let us think of you not merely as the governor of this province, but as the king. You have one son, the prince, whom you love tenderly. Suppose that I am the man who is in debt to the government, owing a sum so vast that I could not pay one part out of a thousand. In accordance with the law, I am cast into prison. Unworthy as I am, your son is a friend of mine: he has a deep interest in me and a real love for me. He seeks you out and says, 'My father, my friend is in prison for a debt which he owes the government, and which he cannot pay. Will you permit me to pay it all for him in order that he may go free?' And you say to him, 'My son, since you are so interested and willing to pay the debt yourself, I am willing that it should be so, and more than that, I will participate with you in it.'

"And so the prince goes to the proper authority and pays my debt in full, leaving nothing to be demanded. He takes the receipt, and comes down to me in my prison cell. I could treat him in three ways. When he comes to me and says, 'Brother, your debt is paid and you may go free,' I could turn in haughtiness and say, 'No; I refuse to be under obligation to anybody,' forgetting that my debt is already an obligation and that I am now only entering into one of lovingkindness, whereas I was before obligated by law. And suppose I continue, 'I will never leave this prison unless I can pay the debt myself.' I would have to remain in the prison, for I could not settle the debt.

"Or I might look at the receipt and say, 'I can't believe it; there is some mistake about it. I can't believe that you would take such an interest in me. I dare not leave; let me remain here. I am afraid to go out lest I be arrested again.' But the prince might say, 'Man, it is foolish for you to talk like that.' And if he should insist on drawing me out of the prison, I would go slinking down the street and trembling as I thought of my debt, and my home would become a prison, for I would be afraid to look out of the window or go to the door. I would have no assurance if I did not believe the message that your son brought.

"But in the third place I could rise up and fall at the feet of the prince, your son, and say, 'I can never repay you for what you have done for me, but I will seek to show by my life how grateful I am to you.' And so I would go free. Let us suppose that on some later day I see the prince riding down one of the streets of the city, and I notice that someone has left a great pile of wood in the street that prevents him from going by. Would I try to get someone to get this out of the way? No, rather I myself would be glad to run out and clear a passage for the prince. If he says, 'Thank you; let me pay for your labor,' I would say, 'Oh, no; you paid my debt; it is a joy for me to do something to show my gratitude.'"

The Turkish governor was listening carefully and watching intently, and suddenly a light shone, and he said, "Oh, then, Dr. Usher, is this the reason why you have a hospital here in Turkey? Is this why you establish these schools and why you missionaries are giving your lives for our people? You are not trying to earn your way into paradise?" "No," said Dr. Usher, "our way into paradise is settled because Jesus has paid the debt, and now we serve because we love Him."

The Turkish governor was thoughtful again and then looked up and said, "You used the illustration of my son paying the debt, and you suggested that God has a Son. But God is one God; He does not beget, and He is not begotten. I cannot accept the idea that God would come down to this world and beget a Son." Dr. Usher said, "But, Your Excellency, when God speaks to us He has to use our language. His thoughts are above our thoughts and His words above our words. We speak to one another in different tongues. If I were to say to you in English, 'In a little while I am going home,' it would mean something altogether different from the message that would be conveyed in Turkish, for in Turkish there is a no word for *home*. I would have to say, 'In a little while I am going to the house.'

But I do not mean that I am going to the building, I mean that I am going to the love of my wife and children whether there is a building or not. That constitutes home for me. And, you see, our poor human language has no word to express the infinite mystery of the relation between the Father and the Son, for it is not such a relationship as you and I know; it is one that existed from all eternity."

The governor felt he could not banish the missionaries, and allowed the work to go on and was himself dismissed from his position because of his grace and kindness in protecting them. They have always hoped that deep in his heart he turned to Christ.

Our Lord saw us in our great need. He paid for us, and having settled the debt He has now brought us into the royal family, washed us from every stain of sin, robed us in garments of glory and beauty, and given us a seat at the table of the King. He has taken us into favor in the Beloved so that the Father's thoughts of Christ are His thoughts of love for us who trust Christ. Out of our appreciation for this, springs the obedience of faith. Out of our gratitude for His love springs the earnest desire to so labor, so work, so live for God that in that coming day when we meet our Savior in glory, we will be acceptable to Him and will hear Him say to us, "Well done, thou good and faithful servant; enter thou into the joy of thy lord" (Matthew 25:21). He does not mean that we enter paradise because of our service, but that entering Heaven in all the infinite value of the Person and work of Christ we share His joy through the ages to come.

Redemption by His Blood (1:7)

In studying the first six verses of Ephesians 1 we have noticed that we were thought of and our happiness planned for by God long before the world began. When the fullness of time had come, He sent the Lord Jesus Christ into the world to carry out His divine purpose. Since His death and resurrection, since His ascension to God's right hand in Heaven, He has accepted us in Christ. In verse 7 we have the assurance of our salvation, "In whom we have redemption." I wish that we might have that firmly fixed in our minds. We do not have to pray, "Take all my guilt away"; we do not have to plead with God to save or to justify us, because these things are blessedly settled and settled for eternity if we have trusted the Lord Jesus Christ. And so we do not hope *someday* to receive the redemption of our soul. We have redemption. We have "redemption through his blood, the forgiveness of sins, according to the riches of his grace."

There are three very distinct words used in the New Testament for *redemption.* One of these words means simply to go into the market and buy—"to purchase"—and when you buy a thing, of course it is yours. We have been bought with a price, the precious blood of the Lord Jesus Christ. We have been redeemed to God by Him and belong to Him. He purchased us; He paid the price for us, made us His own. We sold ourselves for nothing, but we have been redeemed without money.

There is a little fuller word for *redemption,* and this means "to buy out of the market," so that that which has been purchased will never be put on sale again. For instance, in the old slave markets when a slave was bought, the money was paid, and the slave was handed over to the purchaser. In a few rare instances the new owner gave the slave a legal paper, a writ that granted him complete freedom. He was never to be placed in jeopardy again. This is the definition of the word *redeemed* in 1 Peter 1:18:

> Ye were not redeemed with corruptible things, as silver and gold...But with the precious blood of Christ, as of a lamb without blemish and without spot: Who verily was foreordained before the foundation of the world, but was manifest in these last times for you, Who by him do believe in God, that raised him up from the dead, and gave him glory; that your faith and hope might be in God (1 Peter 1:18-21).

We have been "bought out of the market," we are not going to be put on sale any more. We are free.

The third word for *redemption* is the one found in our text. It is a Greek compound, the first part, *apo,* means "away from," going away from something or some condition. The second part, *lutrosis,* means "to be free," "to be loosed," and so it literally means, "to be loosed away from" something. We have been loosed away from the curse of the law that once hung over us. We have been loosed away from the judgment of God toward which we were one time speeding, loosed away from the guilt of our sins. That is why I won't sing, "Take all my guilt away." My guilt was taken away, for we have been loosed away from the entire question of guilt. God will never permit that question to be raised again. It was raised with His own blessed Son at Calvary's cross when all the judgment that my guilt deserved fell on Him, and now I can say:

> Death and judgment are behind me,
> Grace and glory are before;
> All the billows rolled o'er Jesus,
> There exhausted all their power.

It ought to thrill our souls and fill us with a flood of joy continually. No wonder we sometimes sing:

> Redeemed, redeemed, from sin and all its woe.
> Redeemed, redeemed, eternal life to know,
> Redeemed, redeemed, by Jesus' blood!
> Redeemed, redeemed! Oh, praise the Lord!

If we hold our peace when we realize what grace has done on our behalf, the very stones will cry out.

Then notice the price of our redemption—"In whom we have redemption through his blood." No less a price would do; no less a price would have availed to set us free, to deliver us from the curse and the judgment once hanging over us. In Old Testament times the sinner came to the altar bringing a lamb or a goat from the flock, or a bullock from the herd, or if very poor, two turtle doves or young pigeons. These were slain, the blood poured out, and they were offered on the altar and consumed by the fire of divine judgment, a typical sacrifice for sin. But,

> Not all the blood of beasts
> On Jewish altars slain,

Could give the guilty conscience peace
Or wash away its stain.

Isaac Watts

Why? Because there was not sufficient value in those creatures that were offered up through all past dispensations. They did not have intrinsic worth. When that shed blood was sprinkled on the altar and on the sinner, it was powerless to avail, it was powerless to settle the sin question. But, thank God, in our Lord Jesus Christ we see a sacrifice of infinite worth.

People try to reason sometimes as to the extent of His atonement. Some theologians have talked about a limited atonement, for they believe that our Lord made atonement for the elect only, and that outside of that group there is no possibility of salvation for anyone. But let me say this—knowing in my very soul that I have the backing of the Word of God: If every sinner who has ever lived in the world and every sinner who will ever live were to come to God in faith confessing his sin and guilt and putting his trust in the Lord Jesus Christ, so infinite is the value of the work of the cross and the life that was given there, that every sinner could be redeemed from judgment. So precious was the blood that was shed on the cross that every sinner could be freed from every charge, and still there would be untold value in the atonement of Christ, which would avail for the sinners in a million universes like this one. The atoning value of the blood of Jesus cannot be measured.

I remember hearing a Roman Catholic priest say that one drop of the precious blood of Jesus could wash away all the sins that have ever been committed in this world. He was right because on the one hand you have finite sinners, and on the other hand you have the infinite atonement of the Son of God. "We have redemption through his blood." Do you fear then to rest in this wonderful gospel truth? Do you fear then to trust your soul to the Savior who died for your sins on the cross?

Dr. Joseph Parker of London, the noted English preacher, who for many years proclaimed the Word of God in the great City Temple, wrote in his autobiography that there was a time when he gave too much attention to the modern theories of his day. Men were reasoning and speculating and undervaluing the Word of God and he found himself, as he read their books and mingled in their meetings, losing his grip intellectually on the great fundamental doctrine of salvation through the atoning blood of the Lord Jesus Christ alone. But there came into his life the most awful sorrow that he ever had to bear. His devoted wife, whom he loved so tenderly, was stricken, and in a few short hours was snatched away from him.

Dr. Parker wrote that he was unable to share his grief with others, and walking through the empty rooms of his home with a breaking heart, his misery felt for some footing in modern theory and there was none. "And then," he said, addressing a company of his congregational brethren, "my brethren, in those hours of darkness, in those hours of my soul's anguish, when filled with doubt and trembling in fear, I thought of the old gospel of redemption alone through the blood of Christ, the gospel that I had preached in those earlier days, and I put my foot down on that and found firm standing. I stand there today, and I shall die resting on that glorious truth of salvation alone through the precious blood of Christ."

> On Christ the solid Rock I stand;
> All other ground is sinking sand.
> Edward Mote

In what way does the blood of Christ save us? "The life of the flesh is in the blood: and I have given it to you upon the altar to make an atonement for your souls" (Leviticus 17:11). What blood is given on the altar to make an atonement? It is the precious blood of Christ, of which all the sacrifices of the old covenant were simply symbolic. On the cross God gave Jesus, and there He gave up His life when He poured out His blood. It is through the giving of His life, and not through our imitating the life of Jesus, that we are saved. It is through the outpouring of the life of Jesus in the shedding of His blood that we find redemption: "The Son of God, who loved me, and gave himself for me" (Galatians 2:20). And so we have redemption through His blood, and this necessarily involves the forgiveness of sins.

This subject of forgiveness of sins perplexes people sometimes. Forgiveness is presented in Scripture in three very distinct aspects. First, there is *eternal* forgiveness, and that is what the apostle is speaking of in Ephesians 1:7. Every believer is eternally forgiven the moment he comes to God through Jesus. He stands before God justified, every trespass forgiven and as clear before the throne of God as if he had never committed a sin. He never again has to come to God appealing for forgiveness, for He has forgiven all his trespasses. But you may say, "Well, do you mean by that, all my trespasses up to the hour of my conversion?" I mean something far more than that, something far better than that. I mean that the believer's sins, all of them, past, present, and whatever sins may be committed in the future, were all taken into account and were all atoned for when Jesus died. This is the eternal forgiveness of God, the Judge of all. The moment a man trusts in Christ, all the value of that atoning work is put down to his account and every sin is forgiven. That is the first great aspect of forgiveness.

In the second place, there is the *restorative* forgiveness of the Father. The moment my responsibility for my actions as a sinner ended, that moment my responsibility as a child of the heavenly Father began. And if I fail (and I do, and you do) I come to Him not to beg forgiveness, for that was settled at the cross, but I come knowing that, "If we confess ours sins, he is faithful and just to forgive us our sins, and to cleanse us from all unrighteousness" (1 John 1:9). When as a believer I fail, I come to God as my Father and tell Him the story of my failure and my sin. As I confess my sin, it is put away and my communion with the Father is restored. Sin on the part of the believer does not affect his eternal life, for his life is hid with Christ in God, but it does affect his communion with the Father, and that is not restored again until the failing believer comes confessing his sins. Then he receives restorative forgiveness.

The third aspect has been called *governmental* forgiveness. It has to do with the temporal consequences of sin. I think of a Christian man whom I have known for a great many years, who in his unsaved days was given to drunkenness. Though that man lived a wonderful Christian life for over thirty years, he suffered all his life in his body because of his early sins. Sometimes he was tempted to wonder whether God had really forgiven him when the punishment of sin seemed to be going on in his body. Again and again you will find this. God permits temporal punishment to follow sin, but when the believer learns to take everything as from the hand of God and bows to the will of God, He sometimes even grants him governmental forgiveness and restores the body. He may even restore the years the locusts have eaten, and bring back temporal blessings that one might have supposed were lost forever.

On what is His forgiveness based? It is "according to the riches of his grace." It does not say *"out* of the riches of His grace," but *"according* to the riches of his grace." Can you estimate the riches of God's grace? How rich is He in grace? Is He a millionaire? More than that. Is He a multimillionaire? More than that. Is He a billionaire, a trillionaire? More than that. Shall I go on? It is useless, for God's grace is infinite, and you and I have been blessedly saved, forgiven, redeemed, "according to the riches of his grace."

I repeat, it is not merely *out* of the riches of His grace. For example, let us say that you approach a millionaire on behalf of some worthy cause. He listens to you and says, "Well, I think I will do something for you," and he takes out his wallet and gives you a ten-dollar bill. Perhaps you had hoped to receive a thousand dollars from him. He has given you *out* of his riches, but not *according* to his riches. If he gave you a book of signed blank checks all numbered, and said, "Take this, fill in what you need," that would be *according* to his riches.

We who are saved may well rejoice, for we have been forgiven, we have been redeemed, not *out* of the riches of God's grace but *according* to the riches of His grace. If you grasp this thought, you will never feel poor again. And you owe it all to the work of the cross, to the blessed One who there died for you. Through eternity we are going to join with all the redeemed and ascribe all power and praise and honor and glory to the Lamb that was slain, "who redeemed us to God by thy blood out of every kindred, and tongue, and people, and nation" (Revelation 5:9).

May I quote the beautiful words of one of our Christian poets, as emphasizing this precious truth?

O spotless Lamb, my Sacrifice,
Thou art my soul's salvation;
In God's eternal counsel, Thou,
Before the earth's creation,
Wert slain; our God had planned it all
Ere Satan caused Thy creatures' fall
That shrouded them in darkness.
Naught we could do the gulf to span
'Twixt God and sinful fallen man,
Created in God's likeness.

God saw us in our deep, deep need,
He undertook to save us;
'Twas not a trifling thing to Him,
His very best He gave us.
Then mercy's fountain to reveal,
Our weary, sinsick souls to heal,
His Father-heart not sparing,
From Godhead's fullest glory, He
Sent His own Son to earth—I see
Him now my burden bearing.

Oh, love of God, how great and strong
Beyond all human telling!
Oh, wondrous gift! The Father's Son,
All doubt and gloom dispelling,
The Lord of glory come to earth,
A Virgin chosen gave Him birth,
His bed a lowly manger;
Angels adoring hover near,
Shepherds the great glad tidings hear,
But to Thine own a stranger.

In adoration, praise, and love,
My heart is bowed before Thee;
I trust Thy grace, believe Thy Word.
It full assurance gives me

That all my sins are washed away
By Thine own blood! Oh, let me stay
Close by Thy side forever.
I am Thine own, and Thou art mine!
Who from Thy heart and love sublime,
And joy and peace, can sever?

H.A.M.

The Dispensation of the Fullness of Times (1:8-12)

God has many counsels but only one purpose, and that purpose is fully brought before us in these verses. In carrying out this purpose He has His counsels in regard to the people of Israel and to the nations of the Gentiles. "In thee shall all families of the earth be blessed," He said to Abraham (Genesis 12:3). And He has now made known His formerly hidden counsel in regard "to the church, Which is his body, the fulness [completion] of him that filleth all in all" (Ephesians 1:23). He has His counsels in regard to the glorious coming kingdom, when our Lord Jesus will reign over all the earth. But all these are just different parts of His one glorious purpose.

"He hath abounded toward us in all wisdom and prudence." We may think of this first of all as the display of His divine wisdom and intelligence. But there is more than that, there is the subjective side: "He hath abounded *toward us* in all wisdom and prudence." That is, God, through the revelation of His purpose in His Word gives wisdom and knowledge in divine things, which no one else ever had in all the ages of the past. While there were unnumbered saints of God in former dispensations, none had the intelligence in divine things that you and I ought to have today.

Even the angels never had the knowledge of His wonderful plan that the weakest Christian may now have if he will. We are told that angels are learning the wisdom of God in us. He never gave to them a complete revelation of what was coming; but they are learning the wisdom, the counsels, the purpose of God, as they see His grace displayed in us. The church then is an object lesson to angels. It was given to us to understand these things, and not merely for intellectual gratification but in order that the truth might build us up in

Christ, might form us morally and make us what God would have us be. "And every man that hath this hope in him purifieth himself even as he is pure" (1 John 3:3). We are not to view divine mysteries simply as truth on which to exercise our human intelligence; but we are to be sanctified through the truth. The revelation that God has given should so grip our souls and exercise our consciences that it will lead us to behave as a people who are truly strangers and pilgrims here on earth, looking for the glorious era that Christ will bring in when He returns.

"He hath abounded toward us in all wisdom and intelligence"—as the word *prudence* really means. "Having made known unto us the mystery of his will." We need to remind ourselves that the word *mystery*, so frequently used in the New Testament, does not necessarily mean something mysterious or difficult to understand, but rather a secret that no one could understand until it was revealed. The mystery of the kingdom of Heaven (Matthew 13:11), the mystery of lawlessness (2 Thessalonians 2:7), the mystery of Babylon (Revelation 17:5), the great mystery of Christ and the church (Ephesians 5:32), the mystery of the gospel (Ephesians 6:19), the mystery of Israel's present rejection as illustrated in the olive tree of Romans 11—all these were once hidden secrets that no man could understand, but are now opened up to the people of God. So it is the responsibility of a minister of Christ to expound these mysteries to the saints. We read that such are "stewards of the mysteries of God" (1 Corinthians 4:1). From the treasure that God has given them they draw things new and old, and open them up to God's people so that they may understand them.

What is the mystery of His will?

> Having made known unto us the mystery of his will, according to his good pleasure which he hath purposed in himself: That in the dispensation of the fulness of times he might gather together in one all things in Christ, both which are in heaven, and which are on earth; even in him.

Here, succinctly, clearly, in one brief verse, we have the summing up of the mystery of God's will. Everything is working on to this one near-at-hand, divine event toward which the whole creation moves, when God will head up everything in Christ.

What is meant by a "dispensation"? The word *dispensation* is used a number of times in the New Testament, and other words are also used to translate the same Greek word: *stewardship, order, administration.* We find that the original word has been brought right over into English; it is our word *economy.* In other words, "That in the economy of the fullness of times He might head up everything in Christ." What is an economy? An economy is an ordering of a house. But the economy of one house is not necessarily the economy of every other house. If Christians would only bear that in mind, it would save a great deal of confusion. Then there is political economy—the ordering of the affairs of a nation. One nation does not order its affairs in the same way as another. The economy of Russia is not that of the United States of America; the economy of Italy is not the economy of England. These nations have their own ways of ordering their affairs, and if one came from Russia to the United States and attempted to order his conduct according to the economy of Russia, it would not be tolerated here. It might be lawful and right there, but not here. And so there are these various economies running through the Word of God. A dispensation or economy, then, is that particular order or condition of things prevailing in one special age which does not necessarily prevail in another.

There is a difference between a dispensation and an age. An age is a period of time in which a particular economy prevails. There was the economy before the flood when God was dealing with men according to conscience. We do not know just how God's children met and carried on a public testimony in those days. All the information we have concerning that particular time is given us in two or three brief chapters in Genesis. But after the flood, there was a new economy; civil government was instituted by God for the restraint of human conduct. Then we see God calling Abraham out, and making him to be the beginning of a new race of people to whom He entrusted a new economy, the promise of the coming Seed through whom all nations of the earth would be blessed. And then at mount Sinai the law was given to the people of Israel. That economy was in force until our Lord cried, "It is finished," on Calvary's cross.

Now in the present age of the grace of God, we have this wonderful dispensation of the Holy Spirit, in which the gospel of God is being sent out into all the world. There is no one favored nation, but God's grace goes out to all nations. We are not under law as a principle either of salvation or of life, but we are under grace; saved by Christ, kept by Christ, called to walk in Christ to the praise of the glory of His grace. In the future there will be another glorious economy, "The dispensation of the fulness of times." That will be the last glorious age, which has been called ever since the dawn of the Christian era "the millennium" or "the reign of righteousness," when,

> Jesus shall reign where'er the sun,
> Does his successive journeys run;
> His kingdom spread from shore to shore,
> Till moons shall wax and wane no more.
> Isaac Watts

That final dispensation of blessing is not merely for this world, but Heaven and earth will be brought into wonderful unity, and heavenly saints and earthly saints will find their headship in Christ.

How important then that we know something about what God is doing, that we understand intelligently our dispensational place in the ways of God. Many Christians have become confused because, though they are living in this age and are under our special dispensation, they are trying to behave according to another dispensation, confusing law with grace. They are confused because they do not see the difference between God's order for the house of Israel in the Old Testament, and for the house of God, the church in this present age. The church age is to be succeeded by the glorious dispensation of the fullness of times yet to come in the millennium. St. Augustine said, "Distinguish the ages, and the Scriptures are plain."

So God has revealed to us His purpose of grace. He has opened up the good pleasure of His will that we might understand what His plan is for Israel, the church, and the world. What a wonderful time it will be when everything unchristian will be put down, when the authority of the Lord Jesus Christ will be recognized not only by all in Heaven but by all on earth. This is the time referred to in Colossians 1:20: "Having made peace through the blood of his cross, by him to reconcile all things unto himself; by him, I say, whether they be things in earth, or things in heaven." Notice there are only two spheres when Scripture speaks of the future reconciliation. It never includes the sad, unhappy abode of the lost; it simply says that all things in Heaven and all things in earth are some day to be reconciled to God through Jesus Christ.

Scripture also speaks of the subjugation of all things to Christ, "That at the name of Jesus every knee should bow, of things in heaven, and things in earth, and things under the earth" (Philippians 2:10). All created intelligence's will acknowledge the authority of our Lord Jesus Christ. But all in Heaven and all on earth are to be reconciled to Him in the dispensation of the fullness of times, when He will "gather together in one all things in Christ, both which are in heaven, and which are on earth; even in him."

Next we hear Paul speaking as a Jew, as one who belongs to the people to whom the message first came:

> In whom also we have obtained an inheritance, being predesti-nated [marked out beforehand] according to the purpose of him who worketh all things after the counsel of his own will: That we should be to the praise of his glory, who first trusted in Christ [literally, who pre-trusted in Christ] (Ephesians 1:11-12).

The gospel of God was to the Jew first. Those who received the message on the day of Pentecost were all of Israel, although they came from the many different parts of the world into which they had been scattered because of their sins. Wherever the message went it was to the Jew first in those early days, and the apostle Paul, himself a Jew, could speak of the glorious privileges that belonged to them who had become the people of God in Christ. God has made wonderful promises to Israel, to be fulfilled when "they shall see the king in his beauty," and shall cry, "This is our God; we have

waited for him." Israel in that day will be born again and will turn
to the Lord. But Paul said, "We (he and his companions) have already trusted in Christ. We have pretrusted in Him before this day
of His glorious revelation."

"In whom ye [Gentiles] also trusted, after that ye heard the word
of truth, the gospel of your salvation: in whom also after that ye
believed, ye were sealed with that holy Spirit of promise" (13). Paul
first speaks of his fellow-Jews, and then those of the nations who
were alienated and enemies of God.

Notice that the greatest objective then for all Christians is that
which so many of God's beloved people often neglect—the truth of
the coming again of our Lord Jesus Christ. The church's complete
blessing awaits His coming; the redemption of our bodies awaits
His coming; the conversion of Israel awaits His coming; and the
full redemption of all the Gentile peoples awaits the coming of our
Savior. How we should long for this great event, watch for it as one
watches for the morning. Frances Havergal has expressed the
Christian's attitude in a beautiful way:

> Thou art coming, O my Savior!
> Coming, God's anointed King!
> Every tongue Thy Name confessing,
> Well may we rejoice and sing.
> Thou art coming! rays of glory
> Through the veil Thy death has rent,
> Gladden now our pilgrim pathway,
> Glory from Thy presence sent.
>
> Thou art coming! Thou art coming!
> We shall meet Thee on Thy way.
> Thou art coming! We shall see Thee,
> And be like Thee on that day.
> Thou art coming! Thou art coming!
> Jesus, our beloved Lord;
> Oh, the joy to see Thee reigning,
> Worshiped, glorified, adored!

> Thou art coming! Not a shadow,
> Not a mist, and not a tear,
> Not a sin, and not a sorrow,
> On that sunrise grand and clear.
> Thou art coming! Jesus Savior
> Nothing else seems worth a thought:
> Oh, how marvelous the glory,
> And the bliss Thy pain hath bought.
>
> Thou art coming! We are waiting
> With a 'hope' that cannot fail,
> Asking not the day or hour,
> Anchored safe within the veil.
> Thou art coming! At Thy table
> We are witnesses for this,
> As we meet Thee in communion,
> Earnest of our coming bliss.
>   Arr. from Frances R. Havergal

May we understand more and more fully, by reverent, prayerful study of and meditation in the Word of God, the glorious purpose of His grace. And may we walk *now* in the light of that coming dispensation when Christ will see the results of the suffering of His soul and be satisfied!

Sealed with the Holy Spirit (1:13-14)

Next Paul turned to the Gentile converts, therefore the words are especially appropriate as applied to us, "In whom ye also trusted." Notice the change in pronoun, from *we* in verse 12 to *ye*, referring to the Gentiles: "In whom ye also trusted, after that ye heard the word of truth." He was not necessarily implying a lengthy period after they had heard the word of truth. The verse might be translated, "In whom ye also trusted, upon hearing the word of truth." The gospel message believed results in immediate salvation. It is not necessary that people go through a long season of soul-searching and agonizing in spirit after hearing the gospel before they are converted to God. A man may hear the message for the first time, and hearing, believe and live.

Yet one can quite understand the pitiful question of the Chinese woman who had lived in the darkness of paganism all her life. Some itinerant missionaries came to her village, and for the first time she heard the message of grace. She came trembling and said, "It is a wonderful story. I have never heard it before, and you are leaving us tomorrow. I may never hear it again, but I believe it. Do you think once is enough to make my soul secure?" Yes, once is enough!

> Once for all, O sinner, receive it;
> Once for all, O brother, believe it;
> Cling to the cross, the burden will fall,
> Christ hath redeemed us once for all.
> Philip P. Bliss

Most of us have heard this message over and over again. I wonder how many can take these words to ourselves, "In whom ye also trusted, after that ye heard the word of truth, the gospel of your salvation." The gospel is indeed the "good spell." That is the exact meaning of the Anglo-Saxon word, *gospel*. Centuries ago the word *spell* meant "news" or "message." A dynamic orator may be called a *spellbinder* because he can hold an audience with his message. The *gospel* is the "good spell," the "good message." It is God's good news for lost sinners; God's good news about His blessed Son. It cannot be too often emphasized that the gospel is not good advice to be obeyed; it is good news to be believed. And when we believe the message, we are saved.

Now, following our salvation, we are sealed with the Holy Spirit—"In whom also after that ye believed, ye were sealed with that holy Spirit of promise." A good many have been misled by the rendering in the King James version:. "In whom also *after that* ye believed." They have thought that this necessarily implied an interval between believing and being sealed with the Spirit. But I would call your attention to the fact that we have exactly the same words in the previous part of this verse: "In whom ye also trusted, *after that* ye heard the word of truth." A better translation would be, "In whom ye also trusted, *upon hearing* the word of truth." Not necessarily a week or a month, or yet ten minutes after, but *upon hearing*. The same is true in the latter part of the verse: *upon believing* we were sealed with the Holy Spirit.

There is, of course, a difference between the Holy Spirit's regenerating work and the sealing. The difference is as great as that between building a house and moving into it. You may move into it the moment it is ready. When the Spirit of God creates a man anew in Christ Jesus, at that moment a house is built, a temple is prepared, and then the Holy Spirit of God moves in and takes possession of him. "Ye were sealed with that holy Spirit of promise." That is, the Spirit who had been promised in past ages and by our blessed Lord when here on earth, has now come to indwell every believer.

Three times in the New Testament we read of the believer being sealed with the Spirit. We find it here (Ephesians 1:13), and in 2 Corinthians 1:22, "Who hath also sealed us, and given the earnest of the Spirit in our hearts," and then again in Ephesians (4:30), "Grieve not the holy Spirit of God, whereby ye are sealed unto the day of redemption." These are the only three direct references to the sealing of the Holy Spirit in connection with the believer. But in John 6:27 we read that our Lord Himself was sealed: "Labour not for the meat which perisheth, but for that meat which endureth unto everlasting life, which the Son of man shall give unto you: for him hath God the Father sealed." You remember after His baptism in the Jordan, the Spirit of God descended like a dove on Him, and a voice from Heaven said, "This is my beloved Son, in whom I am well pleased" (Matthew 3:17). That is the sealing of the blessed Savior. It is always interesting to note that it is in John 6, where Christ speaks of Himself as the living Bread that came down from Heaven, of which if a man eat he shall live forever, that our Lord also speaks of Himself as sealed.

A seal was a stamp, a mark of ownership, a mark of approval. At one time when you bought a loaf of bread at the grocery store, it had a little stamp on it, or perhaps it had the name of the bakery or the trademark impressed on the bread. This was done by pressing the dough into the pan that had the name in the metal. That name on the loaf of bread is the baker's guarantee. It was as though he said, "I stand back of this bread." It is just so with our blessed Lord. He is the Bread of God, the living Bread, the Bread of Life, and God the Father sealed Him when He gave Him the Holy Spirit. And now when we believe in Him, trust Him as our Savior, the same Holy Spirit comes to live in us. God the Father seals us by the Spirit, and says, as it were, "This man, this woman, belongs to Me; henceforth I stand back of him, I own him as Mine."

It is a remarkable thing that the only two Epistles in which we read of sealing by the Spirit are those written to the Corinthians and Ephesians. Corinth and Ephesus were great centers of the lumber industry in ancient times. A raft of logs would be brought from the Black Sea and notice sent to the different lumber firms that the raft was in the harbor. These firms would send their men out and they would look over the logs and make their selection. One would say, "I will take those logs," another, "I will take these," and they would give a down payment and then cut a certain wedge on each log that the firm had agreed to take. This was called the seal. The logs might not be drawn out of the water for many weeks, but each was sealed by the mark of the firm that had pledged to purchase them.

I was standing on a high bridge at St. Cloud, Minnesota, watching a lumber jam, and as I saw the men working I said to my friend, "Do all these logs belong to one firm?" "Oh no," he said, "there are representatives of many different firms working here in the Minnesota woods." "Well," I asked, "How on earth can they distinguish between the logs?" He showed me from the bridge how they were marked, so that when they reached their destination down the river, the various firms would be able to select their own logs. Though you and I are still tossed about in the waters of this poor world we have been sealed by the Holy Spirit of promise. When the appointed day comes and the Lord takes His own to be with Himself, that will be the day of the redemption of His purchased possession. Then He will take out of this world all who have been sealed with His Spirit. We will go to be with Him in glory.

We may well remember the admonition, "Grieve not the holy Spirit of God, whereby ye are sealed." He who has come to dwell within us will abide with us forever. When the Spirit of God indwells a believer, He never leaves him in life or in death, until the believer is presented faultless in the presence of the glory of our Lord Jesus Christ. The bodies of our beloved dead in Christ are in the keeping of the Holy Spirit, and living saints are indwelt by the Spirit and will be until called to be forever with the Lord.

This enables us to understand the transition of thought as we pass to verse 14. In verse 13 the Holy Spirit is a seal, and in verse 14 He is the earnest, "Which is the earnest of our inheritance until the redemption of the purchased possession, unto the praise of his glory." I mentioned the lumber dealer paying down a small sum as a pledge, the rest to be paid in full when the logs were drawn out of the water. God has given us the Holy Spirit as the pledge that eventually we are to be taken out of this world and fully conformed to the image of His Son. Now we are privileged to appropriate in a small measure what we will have in all its fullness when we get home to Heaven.

> If here on earth the thoughts of Jesus' love
> Lift our poor hearts this weary world above,
> If even here the taste of heavenly springs
> So cheers the spirit, that the pilgrim sings,
> What will the sunshine of His glory prove?
> What the unmingled fullness of His love?
> What hallelujahs will His presence raise?
> What but one loud eternal burst of praise?

What will it mean when we see Him face to face, when the last vestige of sin and infirmity will disappear, and we will be like Him for whom we wait? We will be to "the praise of his glory." Think of it! Every sinner saved by grace divine, will add to the glory and satisfaction of the heart of God throughout eternity. It was in order that we might be won for Christ and set apart for Himself, that our blessed Lord came in grace from the throne in Heaven down to the cross of Calvary. He died that He might redeem us to God with His own blood and make us suitable habitations for the Holy Spirit's indwelling.

Paul's First Prayer for the Saints (1:15-23)

We have in this letter two prayers offered by the apostle Paul, not only for the Ephesians but for all the people of God. The first is our present passage and the second is found in chapter three. Notice that he said, "I also, after I heard of your faith in the Lord Jesus, and love unto all the saints, Cease not to give thanks for you, making mention of you in my prayers." He offered his petition for those who were already saved. When people are born of God, one of the first evidences that they posses a new nature is that they feel a sense of dependence on the Lord and begin to pray, first for themselves, and then their hearts go out in intercession for others.

When the Lord sent Ananias to Saul of Tarsus, Ananias objected, saying, "Lord, I have heard by many of this man, how much evil he hath done to thy saints at Jerusalem: And here he hath authority from the chief priests to bind all that call on thy name." But the Lord had said of Saul, "Behold, he prayeth." This was an evidence of a real work begun in the soul of the former persecutor of the church of God. So Ananias went to him in confidence and laid his hands on him, saying, "Brother Saul, the Lord, even Jesus, that appeared unto thee in the way as thou camest, hath sent me, that thou mightest receive thy sight, and be filled with the Holy Ghost," and he commanded him to be baptized (Acts 9:10-17). It is as natural for the renewed man to pray as it is for the natural man to breathe.

Note how the apostle tells the saints of his confidence in them. He had heard with joy of the way they had been growing in grace, of their faith in the Lord Jesus, and love to all the saints. Where faith is genuine, it will always be manifested by love—not merely to our own peculiar group, but love to all the saints. The term *saints* is an all-inclusive one, taking in every individual who has been born into the family of God. Some have an idea that all the saints are in Heaven, but we do not need to pray for those who are in the presence of the Lord. Believers on earth are called saints, and for them we need to make intercession.

Paul prayed for three distinct things, but first he asked, "That the God of our Lord Jesus Christ, the Father of glory, may give unto you the spirit of wisdom and revelation in the knowledge of him."

We have already seen that in verse 3 Paul exclaimed, "Blessed be the God and Father of our Lord Jesus Christ." Because the eternal Son became man for our redemption, it is right to speak of the *God* of our Lord Jesus Christ. Because His relationship is ever that of Son, it is equally right to speak of God as His *Father*. When we think of God as such, we think of Him as Creator, the source of all counsel and wisdom (God is light), and we notice that in this particular prayer the apostle is especially occupied with the counsels or purpose of God. The prayer in chapter 3 has to do with the family relationship. God is love as well as light.

It is very remarkable how exactly divine titles are used in Holy Scripture. Paul prayed, "That the God of our Lord Jesus Christ, the Father of glory" (or excellence)—all glory proceeds from Him, and glory is the evidence of divine excellence—"may give unto you the spirit of wisdom and revelation in the knowledge of him." He does not mean that you must receive the Holy Spirit in some new and second way. If you are a Christian, you have the Holy Spirit dwelling in you, but He who indwells you delights in His special work of revealing the things of Christ to His saints. How does He do that? By giving insight into the truth found in the Word of God. All Scripture is divinely inspired. "Holy men of God spake as they were moved by the Holy Ghost," but the merely natural man reads the Word and sees nothing in it, because he is not acquainted with its Author. The believer who is indwelt by the Holy Spirit reads, and in reading hears the voice of God. So there is all the difference in the world between reading the Bible in a cold intellectual way and reading it in the presence of God, depending on His Holy Spirit to open up its truth to your heart and mind. It is then that He acts as the Spirit of wisdom and revelation, giving the believer light to enjoy precious things never seen before.

Have you not often heard some servant of God expounding the Word in such a way that it touched your heart in wonderful power and blessing? Perhaps you said, "I've read that passage over and over again, and yet I never saw it like that before. I don't understand how it is that when I read the Bible myself I fail to appreciate these things." Often the real trouble is we do not spend enough time in the presence of God, looking to Him to open up His truth to us.

I remember years ago, while my dear mother was still living, I
went home to visit the family, and found there a man of God from
Northern Ireland. I was a young Christian at the time, engaged in
gospel work. He was a much older man, an invalid, dying of what
we then called "quick consumption." He had come out to southern
California, hoping the climate would be of some help to him. But it
was evident that he was too far gone to be recovered to health again.
He lived, by his own desire, in a small tent out under the olive trees
a short distance away from our home. I went out to see him there. I
can remember how my heart was touched as I looked at his thin
worn face in which I could see the peace of Heaven clearly revealed.
His name was Andrew Fraser. He could barely speak above a whisper because his lungs had been weakened, but I still recall how,
after a few words of introduction, he said to me, "Young man, you
are trying to preach Christ; are you not?" I replied, "Yes, I am."
"Well," he whispered, "sit down a little, and let us talk together
about the Word of God." He opened his well-worn Bible, and in a
simple, sweet, and earnest way he unveiled truth after truth as he
turned from one passage to another, in a way that my own spirit had
never understood.

He spoke until his strength was almost gone. Before I realized it,
tears were running down my face, and I asked, "Where did you get
these things? Could you tell me where I could find a book that would
explain them to me? Did you learn these things in some seminary or
college?" I shall never forget his answer. "My dear young man, I
learned these things on my knees on the mud floor of a little sod
cottage in the north of Ireland. There with my open Bible before
me, I used to kneel for hours at a time, and ask the Spirit of God to
reveal Christ to my soul and make clear His Word to my heart. He
taught me more on my knees on that mud floor than I ever could
have learned in all the seminaries or colleges in the world." It was
not many weeks after this that Mr. Fraser was absent from the body
and present with the Lord, but the memory of that visit has always
remained with me and is a most precious recollection. Is it not true
that most of us do not stay long enough in the presence of God? We
do not get quiet enough to let Him talk to us and reveal His mind to
us.

"Meditation," someone has said, "is becoming a lost art in our day." Another word meaning "meditate" is *ruminate*, which also means "to chew the cud." Just as the cattle take their food in the rough and then ruminate and get the sweetness and the nourishment out of it, so the believer needs to read the Word and then spend time quietly in the presence of God, going over it again and again, ruminating, chewing it, until it becomes truly precious to his heart.

The Israelites of the Old Testament were forbidden to eat the flesh of any animal that did not chew the cud and have a split hoof (Leviticus 11:3). The split hoof is a foot that rises above the filth of this world. It has been well said that it is a great thing when the mouth and the foot agree—when we feed on the Word and walk in the power of its truth. It is when we get into the presence of God that the Holy Spirit delights to show us divine things that we may grow in the knowledge of Christ. That is one reason why the Spirit came.

Every believer to a certain extent has the knowledge of Christ, but the original word *knowledge* in Ephesians 1:17 (KJV) implies more than that. It is not merely knowledge as such; it is really super knowledge, or full knowledge: "That the God of our Lord Jesus Christ, the Father of glory, may give you the Spirit of wisdom and revelation in the *full knowledge* of Him." Perhaps you know Him as your Savior, as the One who has redeemed you from everlasting destruction, as glorious Head of the church, with whom you are linked by the Holy Spirit. He would have you to know Him even better, for there are riches in Christ that you may be sure you have never yet enjoyed. We cannot afford to be negligent, or to let other things crowd out the blessing we might have by giving more time to the teaching of the Holy Spirit.

> Oh the pure delight of a single hour
> That before Thy throne I spend,
> When I kneel in prayer, and with Thee, my God,
> I commune as friend with friend.
> > Fanny J. Crosby

We sometimes sing these words rather glibly. How much do we

know of the reality of spending an hour in His presence, learning more of Him as the Spirit of God unfolds precious truths that otherwise our hearts would never understand?

We have already remarked that there are three distinct petitions in Paul's prayer as recorded in Ephesians 1:18-19. He asked,

1. "That the eyes of your [heart] being enlightened; that ye may know what is the hope of his calling."

2. "And what the riches of the glory of his inheritance in the saints."

3. "And what is the exceeding greatness of his power to us-ward who believe, according to the working of his mighty power."

Our King James version reads, "The eyes of your understanding" (18). But it was not merely the intellect Paul had in view, it was the heart. A better translation of this verse would be, "That the eyes of your heart being enlightened." Christians understand with their hearts. It is "with the heart man believeth unto righteousness." It is with the heart that we grasp divine realities. One may be very brilliant intellectually, but that does not guarantee for a moment that he will have an understanding of spiritual things. It is only as the heart is exercised before God, as the eyes of the heart are opened, that spiritual things will be discerned. That is one reason why people must be born again, otherwise they cannot understand the things of God.

Perhaps an illustration will help to make clear what I mean. Some people are born into the world with a remarkable musical sense, and some have none at all. Now a man who is tone-deaf cannot become a musician, no matter how others may seek to instruct him. Such an one might go to listen to the most wonderful oratorio, but it would all be meaningless to him. He would really have to be born again, as it were, in order to appreciate music, and so in regard to spiritual things, one must have a new nature if he would enter into them appreciatively.

But if the eyes of the heart are opened, then one may understand something of "the hope of his calling." Do you understand what is meant by "the hope of his calling"? It is that to which we have already had our attention drawn in the earlier part of the chapter: "[He] hath blessed us with all spiritual blessings in heavenly places in Christ: According as he hath chosen us in him before the foundation of the world that we should be holy and without blame before him" (3-4). This is the hope of His calling; that some day we will see Him as He is and be like Him. Our God has chosen us for this, and he is never going to give up until we attain to the full stature of men and women in Christ Jesus.

In the second place Paul prayed that we may know "the riches of the glory of his inheritance in the saints." Earlier in the chapter we read of the riches of His grace; here we have the riches of His glory. We are enjoying the riches of His grace now and we will enter into and enjoy the riches of His glory in the future. Notice this expression, "The riches of the glory of his inheritance in the saints." What does that mean? It does not mean that the saints are His inheritance, as some would have us believe, but it does mean that when He takes possession of His inheritance, He is going to take possession of it through His saints. It is not our inheritance in Him, but His inheritance in us. In the Old Testament the land of Canaan was His inheritance, but He took possession of it through His people Israel. Someday He will take possession of a redeemed universe through His saints and we will reign with Him. Who can truly understand our part in that glory?

Then observe Paul's third petition: "What is the exceeding greatness of his power to us-ward who believe, according to the working of his mighty power." You see, Christians are not storage batteries. How often we hear people praying, "O God, give me more power," and you would think that we were a little bit like flashlights that you can open up and put a battery in, then press a button and get a light. You would imagine that as Christians, the Lord puts a power battery into us, presses a button, and then we shine for Him. Nothing of the kind! We have power only as we are living in fellowship with Him who is the source of all power. As we are walking in fellowship with Him, the same power works in and through us that worked in Christ when God raised Him from the dead. That was the fullest demonstration of divine power the world has ever known.

Paul does not call our attention to the power that created the heaven and the earth, to the power that brought the people of Israel out of Egypt, parted the Red Sea, and led them in triumph to the land of Canaan. Nor does he call our attention to the working of mighty miracles through the Lord and His apostles, but to the greatest manifestation of the power of God—the resurrection of the Lord Jesus Christ. This is the same power that works in believers who walk in fellowship with Him:

> According to the...mighty power, Which he wrought in Christ, when he raised him from the dead, and set him at his own right hand in the heavenly places, Far above all principality, and power, and might, and dominion, and every name that is named, not only in this world, but also in that which is to come (1:19-21).

By the expressions, "principality," "power," "might," "dominion," we are to understand the countless hosts of angelic beings, glorious sinless spirits serving our Lord, and also crowded ranks of evil angels opposed to God and His Christ.

Our Lord went down into the depths, into the grave, descended into the lower parts of the earth, and Satan and his hosts rejoiced when they saw Him under the power of death. But God raised Him from the dead, lifting Him to His right hand in the highest glory, where as man He sits today enthroned. That wonderful resurrection power is the focus of the apostle's prayer here. That is the power at work in us as believers if we do not hinder it by our frivolity and worldliness. Do not, I beg of you, ever complain again that you have no power to meet temptation, that you have no power to rise above some sinful habit. If you find yourself in that condition it is because you are out of fellowship with God. Get right with Him; judge the sin that has hindered communion. Then, just as when you make the electrical connection the power flows through the wire to operate the mighty machinery, so you will be living in touch with God, and divine power will work in and through you to enable you to triumph over sin and live to His glory.

We are told that Christ has gone up "above all principality, and power, and might, and dominion, and every name that is named, not only in this world, but also in that which is to come." And then we are told that He has "put all things under his feet" (22). We do not yet see everything subject to Him, but we do see Him seated in the heavenlies above all things, as evidence that all will eventually acknowledge His rightful rule.

Then we have an added word that was never revealed in Old Testament times but is now made known in this dispensation of grace: "And gave him to be the head over all things to the church, Which is his body, the fulness of him that filleth all in all." A head without a body is incomplete. The marvelous thing is that the church is the completeness of Christ. During this present time He is revealing Himself to the world through His church. Some day the members of the body will be with the Head in the glory, and the one new man will be revealed in all his perfection. Is it not a wonderful thing then to realize this: that our Lord would in this sense be incomplete without us? Think of it! We were poor lost sinners of the Gentiles, deserving nothing but the judgment of God, but now through His grace we have been saved, and not only that but made members of His body—the body of Christ—the completeness of Him that filleth all in all. What a hallowed responsibility this puts on us to represent Him aright in this world; to show His grace, His holiness, His love, His hatred of sin, His compassion for the sinner, His desperate earnestness to reach lost men and make known to them the riches of His grace. We are left here to carry on His work in the world where He was crucified. May God move us to rise to a proper sense of our hallowed responsibility and so to make Him known as we should.

EPHESIANS 2

The Christian's Past, Present, and Future (2:1-7)

While holding meetings in Southern California I took public transportation one Saturday to go from Los Angeles to a well-known beach resort. We had hardly left the city when a rather peculiar-looking woman attired in what looked like red bandanna handkerchiefs pieced together, with a shawl on her head and a lot of spangles over her forehead, came and sat down beside me. She asked, "How do you do, gentleman? You like to have your fortune told?" I said, "Are you able to tell my fortune?" She held out a winsome little palm and said, "Cross my palm with a silver quarter, and I will give you your past, present, and future." "You are very sure you can do that if I give you a quarter?" I said, "You see, I am Scotch, and would hate to part with a quarter and not get proper exchange for it." She looked bewildered for a moment, but then said very insistently, "Yes, gentleman, I can give you your past, present, and future. I never fail; I have wonderful second sight. Cross my palm with a quarter. Please, gentleman. I will tell you all." I said, "It is really not necessary, because I have had my fortune told already, and I have a little book in my pocket that gives me my past, present, and future." "You have it in a book?" she said. "Yes, and it is absolutely infallible. Let me read it to you," I said, and I pulled out my New Testament.

She looked startled when she saw it, but I turned to Ephesians 2 and said, "Here is my past: 'And you hath he quickened, who were dead in trespasses and sins: Wherein in time past ye walked according to the course of this world, according to the prince of the power of the air, the spirit that now worketh in the children of disobedience: Among whom also we all had our conversation in times past in the lusts of our flesh, fulfilling the desires of the flesh and of the mind; and were by nature the children of wrath, even as others.'"

"Oh, yes," she said; "it is plenty, I do not care to hear more." "But," I said, as I held her gently by the arm, "I want to give you my present also: 'But God, who is rich in mercy, for his great love wherewith he loved us, even when we were dead in sins, hath quickened us together with Christ, (by grace ye are saved;) And hath raised us up together and made us sit together in heavenly places in Christ Jesus.'"

"That is plenty, gentleman," she said; "I do not wish to hear any more." "Oh but," I replied, "there is more yet, and you must hear it; and you are not going to pay me a quarter for it either. I am giving it to you for nothing. It is my past, my present, and my future. Here is the future: 'That in the ages to come he might show the exceeding riches of his grace in his kindness toward us through Christ Jesus.'"

She was on her feet, and I could not hold on any tighter lest I would be charged with assault and battery, and she fled down the aisle, saying, "I took the wrong man! I took the wrong man!"

People are very interested in trying to delve into the mysterious and unknown. If it were not for this bump of curiosity that so many have, these fortune tellers and spirit mediums, who can tell you how to make immense sums of money but are themselves as poor as church mice, would all die of starvation. People want to know the things that God has not revealed. But it is amazing to see how indifferent they are to the very important revelation that He has given us in His Word. He has made known the past, the present, and the future of the universe, of the nation of Israel, of the great Gentile nations, of the church of God, and then—that which strikes home to every Christian—of every individual believer in the Lord Jesus Christ.

In the King James version we read, "And you hath he quickened." You will notice that the words, "hath he quickened," are in italics. That means that they do not appear in the original Greek text, but were added here to make the sentence read smoothly. The verb *hath quickened* appears in the fifth verse in the original manuscripts. To be quickened is to be made alive. Because we were dead we needed to receive divine life.

"You hath he quickened, who were dead in trespasses and sins: Wherein in time past ye walked according to the course of this world." What a past! We were utterly beyond any ability to save ourselves, for a dead man can do nothing to improve his condition, and every unsaved person is dead, dead toward God, dead spiritually. If you are out of Christ, you have never had one heartbeat toward God; you are dead in trespasses and sins. Sin has not only made man guilty so that he needs forgiveness, but sin has sunk the human race into a state of spiritual death so that men need divine life. That is why we must be born again. Being born again is receiving new life from God through faith in the Lord Jesus Christ.

Of course, there are moral degrees of sinfulness. We would not for a moment say everybody is just as corrupt, just as vile, just as wicked, just as despicable, as everybody else. That would not be true; and yet if people are dead, they are dead. The beautiful little maid, the daughter of Jairus, had been dead only a few minutes when the Lord reached her father's house. But she was dead; she was lifeless. No doubt she was lovely to look upon, especially in the eyes of her beloved parents, like a beautiful marble statue, but although her body had not begun to decay she was dead nevertheless. In Luke's Gospel we find that as the Lord came to the village of Nain a young man was being carried out to be buried. He was dead perhaps a day or two. In the land of Palestine they generally bury the dead either on the day that life ceases or the day immediately following. So this young man was dead longer than the little maid, but life was just as truly extinct in her case as in his. Then we see Jesus at the grave of Lazarus. The sisters told Him not to roll the stone away, for their brother had been dead four days and his corpse would already be offensive. Corruption had set in, but the Lord Jesus brought new life to that man. In every instance it took exactly the same mighty, quickening power to restore the dead.

Only the Son of God could speak life to the daughter of Jairus, to the young man of Nain, and to Lazarus. So we were dead, every one of us who are now saved. Some were deeply corrupted because of sin, others perhaps did not know so much of its vileness and corruption, but all alike were dead before God and needed new and divine life.

"Dead in trespasses and sins." Notice the difference between the two expressions. Sinning is missing the mark. Trespassing is the violation of a definite law. We see the sign "No trespassing" and know that that means we cannot pass a certain boundary without being guilty of transgressing. You and I are guilty on both counts. We are sinners, for we have taken our own way; and we are trespassers because we have actually transgressed what we knew to be the revealed will of God. So we are dead to God in our natural condition. Yet we are able to walk—"Wherein in time past ye walked according to the course of this world." We were dead toward God and could not take one step with Him.

Dr. Gaebelein relates that he was holding meetings in a YMCA auditorium, and one day he was shown a card that the YMCA secretary was in the habit of handing out. It read, "I promise faithfully henceforth to lead a religious and Christian life," and then there was a place to sign one's name. The secretary said, "How do you like that? Isn't that a pretty good way of putting it?" Dr. Gaebelein said, "How on earth can a dead man live any kind of a life? What is the use of putting a card like that into the hands of a dead sinner, and having him sign it and say, 'I promise faithfully henceforth to lead a religious and Christian life'? You cannot live a life for God until you receive a life from God."

You can live according to the world, live a moral life and even what some people call a religious life, but that is only "according to the course of this world." For, after all, the world admires morality and religion. If you are a young man looking for a wife, you do not look in the worst part of the city for some wretched characterless girl. You try to find one who has a bit of religion and morality. And a young woman looking for a husband does the same. People have an idea that morality and religion are necessarily Christian. Of course a Christian ought to be characterized by both, but from a much higher motive than the world. The course of this world is often a religious and a moral course, but apart from Christ.

A little group of Greek philosophers were talking together five hundred years before Christ, and the question was asked, "What is the briefest possible definition of a man?" Plato said, "Man is a two-legged animal." One of them went out, and brought in a rooster. He held him up and said, "Behold Plato's man!" Then one exclaimed, "I have it; man is a religious animal." That is it. There is not another creature in the world but man that ever lifts his eyes toward God and Heaven, that ever feels a sense of responsibility to a higher power, and therefore man is incurably religious. Even the atheist is incurably religious. He worships himself, he is his own god. So, we say, the course of this world may be a religious and a moral course. On the other hand, it may be a vile, abominably wicked, sinful course, but it is all the same—"the course of this world." That is the course in which we walked before we were born again.

"According to the prince of the power of the air." This is, of course, the devil. When living in our sins, the devil was our master and we were led by his will.

"The spirit that now worketh in the children of disobedience [those who refuse obedience to God]; among whom also we all had our conversation [our manner of living, our desire] in times past in the lusts of our flesh, fulfilling the desires of the flesh and of the mind." We sometimes think of the word *lust* as though it referred only to one degrading kind of sin, but it means unlawful desire of any kind. There are just as truly lusts of the mind as lusts of the flesh. Pride, vanity, self-will, covetousness, independence of God——these are all lusts of the mind, and they are just as vile in the sight of God as the lusts of the flesh. In the first three chapters of the Epistle to the Romans we have God's picture of the lusts of the flesh, and in the first three chapters of First Corinthians we have God's picture of the lusts of the mind. One kind is just as sinful as the other.

"And were by nature the children of wrath, even as others." That is, we were born in sin. We were born of a race that is unclean, unholy, and obnoxious to the eyes of God. But God had purposes of grace and of lovingkindness, which He has carried out through Christ Jesus, for the salvation of that sinful race.

Do you recognize the picture of your past? Maybe this is your present instead of your past. If it is, God grant that it may become your past, and that you will be through with this kind of life forever. True life is found alone in Christ.

Now look at the present as described in Ephesians 2:4-6. "But God," what meaning that expression carries. We have God intervening. We were dead, helpless, unable to do one thing to retrieve our dreadful circumstances, but God came in. In creation God came in when this world was "without form and void; and darkness was upon the face of the deep...And God said, Let there be light: and there was light." So when we were dead in trespasses and sins, God came in and spoke the word of living power.

"But God, who is rich in mercy..." In what is He not rich? We saw in Ephesians 1 that He is rich in grace and rich in glory, and here we read that He is rich in mercy. There are infinite resources of mercy for the vilest sinner. There is no one for whom there is no mercy. "God, who is rich in mercy, for his great love wherewith he loved us"—it all came out of the heart of God. There was not a thing about us to commend us to God but, "God so loved the world, that he gave his only begotten Son, that whosoever believeth in him should not perish, but have everlasting life."

> In this was manifested the love of God toward us, because that God sent his only begotten Son into the world, that we might live through him. Herein is love, not that we loved God, but that he loved us, and sent his Son to be the propitiation for our sins" (1 John 4:9-10).

Because we were dead, He sent Jesus to give us life; because we were guilty, He sent Jesus to be the propitiation by bearing our sins in His own body on the tree.

"God, who is rich in mercy, for his great love wherewith he loved us, Even when we were dead in sins, hath quickened us together with Christ" (Ephesians 2:4-5). The whole human race is dead in trespasses and sins. The Jewish part of the race had the revelation from God, and yet they sought to be justified on the basis of works. But these were dead works, and the Jews were just as truly dead in trespasses and sins as the Gentiles, the great godless world outside. But now God comes in and works in power. By the living Word He speaks to the dead Jews and Gentiles, and the Word brings life, and they believe it and are together given new life. They who had been separated before, between whom was a middle wall of partition, are become one in Christ Jesus. That is the meaning of this word *together*. God breaks down the barriers separating Jews and Gentiles and makes them one in Christ through believing, giving us life together *with* Christ, not merely *in* Christ. Why does He put it that way? There was a time when because of my sins Jesus Christ lay dead in the grave, but having completed the work that saves, God made Him alive and brought Him back in triumph from the tomb. Christ's resurrection is the promise of ours. We believe in Him and are brought forth from the place of the dead and quickened with Him. He is the Savior, we are the saved, and together we form one blessed company of which He is now the glorified Head.

"By grace ye are saved," and grace precludes all thought of merit. We were not saved because we prayed so earnestly, repented so bitterly, turned over a new leaf, made restitution for past sins, tried to do good, kept the law and obeyed the sermon on the mount, or anything else that we could do. We were saved by grace, and grace is God's unmerited favor to those who deserve the opposite.

A great many people become upset when they are told that if they were saved once they are saved for all eternity. They imagine that when they come to Christ, it is just the beginning and that they are really on probation. They think that if they keep on and are good enough, they will be saved at last. We are not *being saved*. It is a settled thing. No one is saved for a time and then becomes unsaved, because in order to become unsaved you would have to become unborn, and how can that be? A saved person has been made alive from the dead, born into the family of God, given a new life, and that life is eternal. If that life could ever be forfeited, it would only be probationary life, dependent on one's ability to keep it. I have eternal life, and it is not dependent on my obedience but on the living Christ to see me through to the very end. Do not ever say you are saved if you do not mean that you are saved for eternity. If people ask you if you are saved and you believe you will be saved at last, you will have to say, "Well, not yet; but I hope to be if God and I can only hold out together!" But if you have already trusted the Lord Jesus and believe the Word, say, "Yes, thank God, I am saved for eternity through the precious, atoning blood of the Lord Jesus Christ."

It is one thing to be saved and have eternal life, but it is another thing to be presented before God in all the perfection of His holy Son. It is this of which we read in Ephesians 2:6, "And hath raised us up together, and made us sit together in heavenly places in Christ Jesus." Notice the phrase "in Christ Jesus." Some day we will be caught up and will be *with* Christ, but that will be when we all get home to glory. While still here, God sees us *in* Christ. We are represented by Him and in Him. When the high priest of the old covenant entered the holy place he carried the names of the Israelites on his breast and on his shoulders and they were all seen in their high priest. In the same way, we are seen in Christ, and every moment of our lives He is giving us a perfect representation before the throne of God. I am just as truly raised up together and sitting in heavenly places in Christ Jesus when I am lying flat on my back in the hospital as I am when in church. God sees me up there in Christ. This is a blessed fact that is true of every Christian and not dependent on experience. It is a great thing to have our experience correspond with our standing, and that comes through walking in fellowship with Him.

But what about our future? "That in the ages to come he might show the exceeding riches of his grace in his kindness toward us through Christ Jesus" (7). "The ages to come"—that takes us a long way beyond the millennium. The millennium, or the millennial reign of Christ, is "the *age* to come," and here we have "the *ages* to come." That is the Greek expression for eternity. It consists of untold millions of ages running on forevermore. Through all the ages to come God is going to exhibit the exceeding riches of His grace. One of these days I am going to have a part in a great exhibition, when from the ends of the earth there will be gathered together all the redeemed of the Lord. Then God will demonstrate to all created intelligences how it has been the delight of His heart to show great grace to great sinners. That is our future—a future that does not depend on our faithfulness but on the faithfulness of Him who saved us by grace in order that we might show His glories forever.

God's Workmanship (2:8-10)

As I was meditating on Ephesians 2:8 I thought, *What can I write about it that has not been written a hundred times already?* But it cannot be otherwise, for in trying to present the salvation of God one must be reminded of a passage like this over and over again, for that is the very heart of the matter.

Our God jealously guards against the indifferent treatment of the Person and work of His beloved Son. God loves poor sinners so much that He sent His Son into the world to be the atonement for our sins. But He loves His Son so much that He will not permit anyone to enter Heaven who ignores the work that the Lord Jesus Christ accomplished. It is only through His finished work that any of us have a right to a place in Heaven, and so our salvation is entirely by grace. And grace utterly precludes the thought of human merit. Were there any question of merit on our part, it would not be grace. "To him that worketh is the reward not reckoned of grace, but of debt" (Romans 4:4). If you work, you put the one by whom you are employed into your debt, and he does not get out of your debt until he has paid for your labor. Therefore, if by our works or efforts we could earn God's salvation, we would put God in our debt, and He could not get out of it until He had taken us home to Heaven as a reward or payment for what we had done. But no works of ours, no efforts of ours, no labor that we could perform, could ever take away the guilt of one sin; we are confined to grace, to unmerited favor. It is not only unmerited favor, but it is favor against merit, for we have merited the very opposite.

"By grace are ye saved." Notice the apostle does not say, "By grace are ye being saved," or, "by grace will ye be saved eventually," but he is declaring something already true of every believer in the Lord Jesus Christ: the work of redemption is already consummated. Therefore, our salvation is looked at by God as something that is finished and complete. If there were any possibility that somehow along the way to Heaven I might lose the salvation of God, it could not be said that I am already saved, but rather that I am being saved. But thank God, not only is the work that saves finished, but my salvation is seen as an accomplished fact. Verse 8 might be translated, "By grace have ye been saved."

"Through faith," this is the agent. Faith is simply the hand that lays hold of the gift that God presents to me. Believing the gospel, I am saved. Some people are in danger of making a savior of their faith, for they say, "Well, if I could only believe firmly enough, if I could believe in the right way, I think I would be saved." It is not a question of how you believe; it is a question of whom you believe. Paul said, "I know whom I have believed, and am persuaded that he is able to keep that which I have committed unto him against that day" (2 Timothy 1:12). Do not make a savior of your faith. The Savior is Christ, and faith lays hold of Him. Then, lest the redeemed one thinks that he deserves credit for coming to Christ and believing this message, the apostle immediately adds, "And that not of yourselves: it is the gift of God."

Take the message as a whole again, "By grace are ye saved through faith; and that not of yourselves: it is the gift of God." Theologians have questioned as to whether "not of yourselves" means the salvation or the faith. We may apply it to the whole subject in question. The grace, the salvation, is not of yourselves. The faith is not of yourselves; it is all the gift of God. But somebody says, "If faith is the gift of God and God is not pleased to give me that gift, how can I believe?" Scripture says, "Faith cometh by hearing, and hearing by the word of God." God gives the gift of faith to all who heed the message of the gospel. After the Spirit of God brings that message home to the heart, it is thoroughly possible to resist the Holy Ghost. It is possible on the other hand to obey the ministry of the Spirit, and thus be led on to personal faith in the Lord Jesus Christ. Faith is a gift, and apart from it you can never be saved, but in order that we may have faith, "God so loved the world, that he gave his only begotten Son, that whosoever believeth in him should not perish, but have everlasting life." Refuse the Word, and there will never be faith; give heed to the Word, and faith cometh by hearing. And so we may say that all aspects of our salvation are "not of works, lest any man should boast."

John Nelson, one of Wesley's preachers, was a poor, godless, blaspheming blacksmith until God saved him. After that he became one of the early Methodist preachers, proclaiming in power the gospel of the grace of God and winning many to a saving knowledge of the Lord Jesus Christ. One day he was talking to a very self-righteous man who said, "I don't need your Savior; my life is all I need. I can present my own life to God, and I am satisfied He won't be hard on me. If anybody gets into Heaven I will because of the good I have done and the way I have lived." "Look here," said John Nelson, "if you got into Heaven, you would bring discord there. All in Heaven will be saved sinners, and we are going to sing, 'Glory to the Lamb that was slain and hath washed us from our sins in His own blood.' You couldn't sing that, and so you would bring discord. You would be singing, 'Glory to me because by my own good life and consistent living, my charity and good behavior, I fitted myself for Heaven.' If the angels caught you doing that, they would take you by the nape of your neck and throw you over the wall." That is a rather crude way of putting it, but he knew the truth of salvation by grace. David said, "My soul shall make her boast in the Lord" (Psalm 34:2). I have no goodness of my own, no faithfulness, no merit, but I will boast in Him.

In Ephesians 2:10 we read, "For we are his workmanship, created in Christ Jesus unto good works, which God hath before ordained that we should walk in them." The word translated "workmanship" is used only twice in the New Testament. As well as here in Ephesians it is also found in Romans 1 where Paul was speaking of the testimony of creation. He wrote in verse 20, "For the invisible things of him from the creation of the world are clearly seen, being understood by the things that are made, even his eternal power and Godhead; so that they are without excuse." In this verse the phrase, "the things that are made," is the translation of one Greek word, *poiema*. From it we get our English word *poem*. Creation is God's poem, witnessing to His eternal power and glory. The very stars in the heaven are, "Forever singing as they shine, / The hand that made us is divine."

Poiema is used again only in this second chapter of the Epistle to the Ephesians, and here it is translated "workmanship," which means something that someone has made. So we read that, "We are his workmanship [His poem], created in Christ Jesus unto good works."

What a wonderful piece of literature a poem is! How different from any prose! It takes a gifted man or woman to produce a worthwhile poem. It is an artistic creation, and all the hard work in the world would not enable you to produce one unless you have the poetic instinct. It is a very artistic thing to play an organ, and I might take lessons and practice for years but I would never get great music out of it because I have no music in me. If God were other than He is, He never could have brought this universe into existence nor saved one poor sinner. Creation is God's first poem, but redemption is His second poem, and you and I who are saved constitute the syllables in God's great poem of redemption. Everyone is set in the right place by God Himself, "We are his workmanship," and therefore He is given all the credit, for He has done it all through His Son.

We are "created in Christ Jesus unto good works." Notice the order. He has already told us that we are not saved by good works, but now says that we must not ignore good works, for one of the purposes for which He has saved us is that we might do good works. In the general Epistles there are two great "sayings": In 1 Timothy 1:15 we read "This is a faithful saying, and worthy of all acceptation, that Christ Jesus came into the world to save sinners." But in Titus 3:8 we read, "This is a faithful saying, and these things I will that thou affirm constantly, that they which have believed in God might be careful to maintain good works. These things are good and profitable unto men." You see the place good works have, they are not to be ignored, but they are not meritorious. We are not saved by them, but we are created in Christ Jesus *unto* good works. In other words, springing from the fact that we have been saved and have become God's workmanship, God's great redemptive poem, our lives should now be musical—rhythmical and lyrical. Every one of us should fit into the place where He has set us in this great epic of redemption.

"We are his workmanship, created in Christ Jesus unto good works, which God hath before ordained that we should walk in them." Do you believe in foreordination? If you are a Christian, you are foreordained to do good works, to live a life well-pleasing unto God. That is what He has marked out for you. The Christian's pathway is a life lived in obedience to Him.

Made Nigh by the Blood of Christ (2:11-18)

In this passage, the apostle addressed converted Gentiles collectively and spoke of converted Jews collectively. In times past God had called one man, Abraham, out from the world and made him the depository of certain promises. Afterwards He gave to his seed the Mosaic covenant at mount Sinai, and by that God separated the people of Israel from all the other people of the world. Those outside of Israel were called Gentiles. When Christ came into the world and the gospel first began to be preached, it could be said that those who were Gentiles in the flesh, like ourselves, "were without Christ, being aliens from the commonwealth of Israel, and strangers from the covenants of promise, having no hope, and without God in the world."

Israel had a very definite hope. God had promised certain things to them. But the Gentiles had no such hope, they were outside of all this, and therefore without God in the world. It was not merely that they worshiped idols, gods of wood and stone, but the point was they did not know the true God at all. They were godless, "atheists," in the world. But now, through the coming of our Lord Jesus Christ and through His death on Calvary's cross, wondrous blessing goes out to the Gentiles, blessings of which they had never dared to dream in the past.

"Now in Christ Jesus ye who sometimes were far off are made nigh by the blood of Christ" (13). You see the Jew occupied a place of nearness to God through covenant relationship, while the Gentile was far off, being a stranger to it all. But the Jew through his failure to keep his part of the covenant of works, had himself become personally alienated from God, so that in His sight, as we read in the Epistle to the Romans, "There is no difference, For all have sinned, and come short of the glory of God." Therefore, the same grace that flowed out to Israel is the grace that overflows to the Gentiles. The Jews never obtained salvation on the ground of merit, or because they were God's peculiar people marked off from the nations of the world by the covenant of circumcision, nor because of the sacrifices that they offered throughout the legal dispensation. Those of them who were saved owed everything to the matchless grace of God who gave the Lord Jesus Christ, their promised Messiah, to die for their sins on that cross of shame. And that same mighty Sacrifice which was offered on the tree avails for men everywhere who put their trust in Him. And so, although no covenant has been made with the Gentiles, yet every believing Gentile comes under all the spiritual blessings of the new covenant the moment he trusts in Christ, because salvation is all pure grace.

The shedding of the blood of our Lord Jesus Christ was the greatest crime ever perpetrated on the face of this earth. When a man murders another, he is held responsible for taking the life of his fellowman, but when a man stretches forth his hand against God incarnate, what can be said about his guilt! Yet that is the awful crime in which Jews and Gentiles participated. When the Lord Jesus Christ was nailed to Calvary's tree and His blood poured out, it was the demonstration of the world's greatest sin, but it also became the greatest possible demonstration of the infinite love and grace of God. That which exhibited the enormity of man's sin and the corruption of his heart is that which shows the love of God to the greatest extent. All this was foreseen.

Peter could say, "Him, being delivered by the determinate counsel and foreknowledge of God, ye have taken, and by wicked hands have crucified and slain" (Acts 2:23). Yet this same Jesus is now made Lord and Christ, and through Him all who believe, as the apostle Paul says, "are justified from all things." The Roman spear driven into the very heart of the Son of God expressed the wickedness of the heart of man, but that cleansing blood rushing forth to wash away our sins expressed the extent of God's love. How wonderfully the grace of God has abounded over all our sins! We who sometimes were far off, we poor, wretched Gentiles, alienated from God by wicked works, and enemies in our minds, have now, by putting our trust in Him, been brought into a place of nearness that the law could never give even to Jews. And the Jew who believes in Him has been brought into this same blessed place. Together we have been "made nigh by the blood of Christ."

There was not sufficient intrinsic value in the blood of sacrificed beasts to settle the sin question. But in the case of our Lord Jesus

Christ we see the Holy, the Just, the Sovereign of the skies, stooping to man's condition. He had to be who He is in order to do what He did, and because He is the infinite God become man His blood has atoning value that no other blood could have. Thus we are brought near by that blood of Christ. We may well sing:

> So near, so very near, to God,
> Nearer I could not be;
> For in the person of His Son,
> I am as near as He.
>
> So dear, so very dear, to God,
> Dearer I could not be;
> The love wherewith He loves the Son,
> Such is His love to me.

Dear Christian, does your heart grasp this profound truth? Do you realize that the very moment you came, a feeble trembling sinner, and reached out the hand of faith, accepting God's Son, that moment by the precious blood of Christ you were brought into such an intimate relationship with God that you could not be drawn any closer? We are not brought to God by the sincerity of our repentance, by the strength of our faith, by the depth of our devotion, by the gladness of our spiritual experience, but brought near by the blood of Christ. We owe everything for eternity to the precious atoning blood of our Lord, and He who shed that blood, He who died for our sins on the cross, is Himself our peace.

We read, "Being justified by faith, we have peace with God" (Romans 5:1). That peace is not merely an experience of calmness in the soul, but it is the realization that the sin question has been fully settled. The sin that separated our souls from God has been done away, done away in the cross, and so Christ Himself is our peace. You see I am not called on to be mastered by my feelings, but by Christ. I may be very happy today, and then circumstances may arise tomorrow that cause the clouds to overshadow my soul and hide the sunshine of God's face. I may be in darkness, doubt, difficulty, and perplexity, but my peace remains unchanged.

> Peace with God is Christ in glory,
> God is just and God is love;
> Jesus died to tell the story,
> Foes to bring to God above.

And so when I get disgusted with myself and my own poor experience, I can look away from self and look up by faith to Him, the blessed Christ of God seated there on the right hand of the Majesty in Heaven, and say, "There is my peace; my heart rests in Him. God rests in Him, and I rest in Him." Has your soul truly understood this? I hope these things become a practical part of our lives, not merely doctrinal statements, but realities that sink into the depths of our beings.

"For He is our peace, who hath made both one" (Ephesians 2:14). Does Paul mean that God has made Christ and us one? That is blessedly true, but that is not what is spoken of here. He was speaking a little farther back of two opposite groups—the circumcision and the uncircumcision, the Jew and the Gentile, the covenant people and those who are strangers to the covenants of promise. But when Christ died, He died for both, and we who believe from both of these groups are now reconciled to God, and therefore we read, "He hath made both one." And so my Jewish brother and I, his Gentile brother, are one in Christ.

"And hath broken down the middle wall of partition between us." I think the apostle is referring, as an illustration at any rate, to the wall in the old temple, separating the court of the Gentiles from the court of the Israelites. On this wall there was an inscription that was dug up some years ago, and it read, "Let no Gentile, let no man of the nations, go beyond this wall on pain of death." But the apostle wrote, Christ "hath broken down the middle wall of partition between us."

"Having abolished in his flesh the enmity, even the law of commandments contained in ordinances; for to make in himself of twain one new man, so making peace" (15). What does he mean by "one new man"? It is the body consisting of redeemed Jews and Gentiles here on earth and our glorious Head, our Lord Jesus Christ, in Heaven. Redeemed sinners united by the Holy Spirit to Christ in Heaven from now on form one new man, and so in a double sense peace has been made between the individual soul and God, and between Jew and Gentile, once separated by this middle wall of partition. In order that peace might be made between the individual soul and God, the law with its regulations had to be abolished.

That law pronounced a curse and condemnation on all who violated it. It was the Jews' pride and boasting that they were custodians of the law of God, and yet they did not realize that same law put them all under the curse. They thought they were a blessed people and a privileged people to have the law of God, but sadly they had broken the law, and God said, "Cursed is every one that continueth not in all things which are written in the book of the law to do them" (Galatians 3:10). But the Lord Jesus went to the cross and was made a curse for us—"As it is written, Cursed is every one that hangeth on a tree" (Galatians 3:13). And so by enduring the cross, by bearing the judgment, He abolished the law. And now both Jews and Gentiles come to God on the same basis, as sinners, but as sinners for whom Christ died. The redeemed from these two groups comprise the new man of which Christ is the Head.

Then in verse 16 he used the other term, the *body*: "That he might reconcile both unto God in one body by the cross, having slain the enmity thereby." Why not say, "That He might reconcile both unto God in one *new man*"? We read that He has made in Himself of Jew and Gentile one new man. That includes the body on earth and the Head in Heaven. However, Christ does not have to be reconciled to God. It is we, the body, that must be reconciled to Him, for we were all poor sinners, we were once on our way to everlasting ruin, but we have been reconciled to God in one body. How are we reconciled to God? You remember, our Lord came into the world to manifest the love of God to sinners, and we read, "God was in Christ, reconciling the world unto himself." But what was the result? Did men receive Him gladly? Did they acknowledge Him as Savior and Lord? Instead of that they nailed Him to the cross of shame. But love that was stronger than death, love that the many waters of judgment could not quench, led Him to go down into the darkness of the tomb for us. He destroyed the hostility by taking our place on the cross and bearing the judgment for us. Now through faith in the risen Christ who died for our sins, we have been reconciled to God.

"[He] came and preached peace to you which were afar off, and to them that were nigh" (17). In resurrection power, having settled the sin question, having completed the work that makes atonement, the blessed Lord returned to this very world that rejected Him. He appeared here for forty days in His resurrection body, and gave the message of the gospel to His disciples to carry into the world. He proclaimed the good news of "peace to you which were afar off"—Gentile sinners dying in ignorance and darkness—"and to them that were nigh"—Jews to whom His Word had come. The Jews had received the oracles of God and the light that the Gentiles knew nothing of, but they had joined with the Gentiles in crucifying the Lord of glory. In the love of His heart, Christ preached the message of peace to Jews as well as to Gentiles.

In verse 18 we have a wonderful statement: "For through him"—the resurrected Christ who ever lives at God's right hand to make intercession for us—"we both"—Jews and Gentiles who were once far off—now "have access by one Spirit unto the Father." Under the old covenant there was no immediate access to God. The temple curtain told of a God hidden in the dark. God was not able to come out to man because the sin question was not settled, and man could not go into God for there was no way for his sins to be cleansed. But now the death of Christ has torn the separating veil.

> The veil is rent! Our souls draw near
> Unto a throne of grace;
> The merits of the Lord appear,
> They fill the holy place.
>
> His precious blood has spoken there,
> Before and on the throne:
> And His own wounds in heaven declare,
> The atoning work is done.
>
> 'Tis finished! Here our souls have rest,
> His work can never fail:
> By Him, our Sacrifice and Priest,
> We pass within the veil.

Within the holiest of all,
Cleansed by His precious blood,
Before the throne we prostrate fall,
And worship Thee, O God!

Through Christ we both have immediate access to the Father by the
Holy Spirit. This Spirit was given by God at Pentecost, baptizing
believing Jews and Gentiles into one body, making us both members of one new man. What a wonderful thing it is to be a Christian!
What a wonderful thing it is not only to have your sins forgiven but
to have been brought into the family of God, and to have been made
a fellow member with other believers of the body of Christ. Not
only that, but to be accepted by God and to be as near to the heart of
God as His own beloved Son. Not only that, but to have immediate
access at any moment into His presence in the power of the Holy
Spirit. And all this rests on the infinite value of the blood of the
Lord Jesus Christ. We truly are "made nigh by the blood of Christ."

Built Together for a Habitation of God (2:19-22)

Next we consider our relationship to the Holy Spirit, and find
that we have been formed into a habitation in which God by the
Holy Spirit dwells during our time on earth, and in which He will
dwell throughout all the ages to come. Two different figures are
used—the tabernacle as described in the book of Exodus, and the
glorious temple as depicted for us in the books of Kings and
Chronicles. The tabernacle represents the temporary condition, the
temple the eternal condition that will abide forever.

We noticed earlier in our study that throughout this letter the
apostle said "ye" when he was addressing Gentiles and "we" when
he wrote of Jews. So in this verse he said, "Ye are no more strangers and foreigners, but fellow-citizens with the saints, and of the
household of God." We have seen that the Gentiles were "strangers
from the covenants of promise." They did not belong to that special
elect nation of Israel, but sadly many in Israel failed to enter into
their holy privilege, and so we are told elsewhere that they are not
all Israel who are of Israel. However, God called out a remnant

from Israel, and that remnant by accepting the Lord Jesus Christ as Savior was baptized into Jesus Christ and made living stones in the house of God. And now Gentiles who believe, though having no part nor lot in the covenant with Israel, are also brought in and are no longer "strangers and foreigners, but fellow-citizens with the saints."

What do we mean by "saints"? Simply that we are now linked with Israel after the flesh? Not at all. The Israelites forfeited all rights from an earthly standpoint. It is those in Israel who believe in the Lord Jesus Christ who are here called saints. So when he says we are "fellow-citizens with the saints," he means that the Gentiles who believe in the Lord Jesus Christ are as truly united to Christ now by the Spirit as our Jewish brethren who believe in the same Savior. A *saint* is a holy one, one set apart to God. But holiness is not a question primarily of experience. People often think of saints as those who have already attained to perfect holiness, but that is not the divine thought at all. Everyone who puts his trust in the Lord has been set apart to God in Christ, and thus is constituted a saint. But now having been made a saint, one is called to live in a saintly way. We do not become saints by holy living, but because God has designated us saints we are called to holy living.

So we read that we have been made "fellow-citizens with the saints." What citizenship is that? It is a heavenly citizenship. We read in Philippians, "Our conversation [citizenship] is in heaven." Philippi was what the Romans called a colony, but they used that term in a different sense from what we use it today. A Roman colony was a city that had been characterized by some special devotedness to the Roman imperial government. In order to reward the citizens of that place for their loyalty and faithfulness the title *colonia* was conferred on that city. That meant that from that time on every free-born person living in that place was considered a Roman citizen, and had just exactly the same rights and privileges as though he were born free in Rome.

Some years before Paul wrote the letter to the Philippians the Romans were in conflict with the people to the north and to the east of Macedonia. When the Roman legions reached Philippi they found the citizens of that place had already raised a great army to assist them, and had provided vast resources to meet the army. So delighted was the Roman general with their generosity and loyalty that he sent back to Rome a splendid report. The Senate then met and conferred on them the title *colonia*, which meant that every Philippian could then say, "I am a Roman citizen." However, Philippi was in Macedonia, and of course the people had certain duties to that government, but Philippi was governed directly from Rome, and had a representative of the Roman government there. The apostle applied this same concept of citizenship in writing to the Ephesians. We are in this world sinners saved by grace and linked to our Lord Jesus Christ, though He is rejected by this world. And now God so appreciates devotion to His blessed Son in this day of His rejection, that He says, "I am going to confer on everyone who trusts Him, on everyone who acknowledges His Lordship during this time when the world is spurning Him, citizenship in my 'colonia.' They are heavenly citizens; they belong to Heaven." Though we are in the world, we are "fellow-citizens with the saints." We have our duties, our responsibilities to the world in which we live, but our prime duty and responsibility is to Heaven because we are citizens of that blessed country and belong to the household of God.

Next Paul used the figure of a building, and said, "And are built upon the foundation of the apostles and prophets, Jesus Christ himself being the chief corner stone." You remember this same figure is used in other places in the New Testament. In 1 Corinthians 3 we read of the building that God is erecting in the wonderful gospel days. You have it again in 2 Corinthians 6 where we read of the temple of God, and also in 1 Peter 2 where believers are likened to living stones built on *the* living Stone, our Lord Jesus Christ.

In the Old Testament when Solomon's temple was erected on mount Moriah, in order that there might be a level platform on which the great superstructure could stand, large stones were brought and mortared into the solid rock, and then stones were fitted into that temple. At the end of seven years it was the most wonderful sanctuary that the world had ever known up to that time. But there was a peculiarity about the construction. It went up without the sound of a hammer, because the stones were quarried out elsewhere. They were also cut, shaped, and polished elsewhere, and then placed on that platform and cemented together without the use of a workman's hammer. So today no one can hear a sound as a living stone is fitted into the temple of God, but God by the Holy Ghost is quarrying out these living stones from the depths of sin. He is lifting them up by His mighty power and building them on Christ, the great foundation.

> View the vast building, see it rise!
> The work how great, the plan how wise!
> Nor can that faith be overthrown
> That rests upon the Living Stone.

Some day this temple will be completed, but it is now in the course of construction. Every believer is a living stone. In Africa, India, China, and the islands of the sea, God is finding these living stones and they are being built into this glorious structure. It will remain for eternity the glorious sanctuary in which God will display the riches of His grace to all people. What a wonderful thing to be a living stone in that temple! You see no man can make himself a living stone. Only the Spirit of God can do that, and therefore it is only those who have believed in the Lord Jesus Christ who are placed in this wonderful building.

"And are built upon the foundation of the apostles and prophets, Jesus Christ himself being the chief corner stone." Does Paul mean that the apostles and prophets are the foundation? Not at all. He means God's temple is built on the foundation that the apostles laid. What foundation did they lay? Paul wrote, "Other foundation can no man lay than that is laid, which is Jesus Christ" (1 Corinthians 3:11). So the apostles and the prophets proclaimed the truth of the Lord Jesus Christ, and on that foundation this glorious temple is being built.

You say, "But what prophets was Paul speaking of? We have no difficulty with the apostles for we know they are the apostles of the new dispensation. Do the prophets include the Old Testament prophets?" We answer, They preached Christ. Who preached a more glorious gospel than Isaiah? Listen to His wonderful words, "He was wounded for our transgressions, he was bruised for our iniquities:

the chastisement of our peace was upon him; and with his stripes we are healed" (Isaiah 53:5). Listen to Jeremiah, "This is his name whereby he shall be called, the Lord our Righteousness" (Jeremiah 23:6). Listen to Zechariah, "Awake, O sword, against my shepherd, and against the man that is my fellow, saith the Lord of hosts: smite the shepherd, and the sheep shall be scattered: and I will turn mine hand upon the little ones" (Zechariah 13:7). And so we might go on. In this sense the prophets of the Old Testament joined with the apostles of the New Testament in proclaiming the truth of a crucified and risen Savior. But if he had in mind these Old Testament prophets, we might expect him to say "prophets and apostles," for these Old Testament prophets came long before the apostles did. But he reversed it and put the apostles first. Could it be that just as there were apostles in the New Testament dispensation, there were also prophets? We read, for instance, of certain prophets and teachers at Antioch (Acts 13:1). Some of the writers of the New Testament, as Mark and Luke, were not apostles but were prophets. So I take it that we are to limit the "apostles and prophets" of Ephesians 2:20 to the New Testament workmen, those who were raised up of God at the beginning of the church age to lay the foundation—to preach Christ and proclaim the gospel. The temple of God has been building through the centuries on this glorious proclamation.

"Jesus Christ himself being the chief corner stone." "There is none other name under heaven given among men, whereby we must be saved" (Acts 4:12). Christ is the one Mediator between God and man. Only those who put their trust in Him are built into this holy temple. Only those who have been saved through His death, His shed blood, and His glorious resurrection are members of His body. Only those who have rested their souls for eternity on the work that He accomplished at Calvary have been quickened together with Him and are thus brought into the family of God. These are our brethren. Others are our fellowmen, in whom we are deeply interested, over whom we yearn with the compassion of Christ. But we dare not take that sacred term of "brethren" and apply it to those who reject our Lord Jesus Christ and trample His blood under their feet, for it is on His work alone we rest.

We remember Christ said to Peter, "Whom say ye that I am?"

and Peter answered, "Thou art the Christ, the Son of the living God." Jesus said, "Blessed art thou, Simon Bar-jona: for flesh and blood hath not revealed it unto thee, but my Father which is in heaven. And I say unto thee, That thou art Peter, and upon this rock I will build my church." This is the one foundation. It was laid in death when Jesus died on the tree and now in resurrection the Spirit is building this glorious temple on Christ.

But now, as we said, the temple is not yet finished. As long as there are still lost sinners to be brought in, the temple is not complete. If you should ask for my opinion as to how near we are to the finished temple, I would say that I think there are very few more stones to be put in, just one here and there in the roof, and then it will be complete.

"In whom all the building fitly framed together groweth unto an holy temple in the Lord." That is, every one is fitted by the Holy Spirit into his or her exact place as a living stone. It is an ongoing process. And when it is all completed, what a dwelling place for God and the Lamb it will be. What a wonderful sanctuary through all the ages to come! When you think of being a living stone in that glorious building, does it not bring to your soul a sense of the importance of holy living and devotedness to Christ, of so behaving yourself that He will delight in dwelling in you?

In 1 Corinthians 3 and 2 Corinthians 6 the temple of God is the entire church, but in 1 Corinthians 6 the temple of the Holy Spirit is the individual. In 1 Corinthians 3:16 we read, "Know ye not that ye are the temple of God, and that the Spirit of God dwelleth in you?" And then speaking of the enemies outside, Paul continued, "If any man defile the temple of God, him shall God destroy; for the temple of God is holy, which temple ye are." In 2 Corinthians 6:16 we read, "What agreement hath the temple of God with idols? for ye are the temple of the living God; as God hath said, I will dwell in them, and walk in them; and I will be their God, and they shall be my people." And it is because the church collectively comprises the temple of God that the command comes, "Wherefore come out from among them, and be ye separate, saith the Lord, and touch not the unclean thing; and I will receive you" (17). But when we look back

at 1 Corinthians 6:19 we find that Paul changed the figure to the
individual. "What? know ye not that your body is the temple of the
Holy Ghost which is in you, which ye have of God, and ye are not
your own?" Here we find he used the singular form—"your body,"
not "your bodies." The individual is the temple of the Holy Ghost,
which is in him. Addressing the whole company he said that collectively they form the temple of God but each individual believer's
body is the temple of the Holy Ghost. What godliness should characterize us, what piety and separation from the world: what faithfulness to Christ should mark us!

Coming back to Ephesians 2:20-21, the temple is spoken of, but
in verse 22 we have, I believe, the thought of the tabernacle. He has
been speaking of the whole company of believers, and now he nar-
rows his attention down to address a specific group of believers,
like this church at Ephesus. "In whom ye also are builded together
for an habitation of God through the Spirit." That is a finished prod-
uct right here on the earth, like the tabernacle that could be placed
at a given place one day, taken down the next, and moved elsewhere. It was made of a number of boards that had been fitted together, covered with gold, and united by bands. Then on each board
there were two tenons which went down into sockets of silver. Beautiful curtains covered the united framework. At one time those boards
had been trees in the wilderness, as you and I were poor sinners
having no hope in the world. Then we were cut down by the work
of the Spirit of God, planed and fitted together by the Spirit and
now made the abiding place of God. The boards were covered with
gold—symbolic of the fact that we are made the righteousness of
God in Christ. The curtains speak of all His perfections sheltering
His own. This is the picture that is given to us in Ephesians. You as
a company of Christians are builded together for an habitation of
God through the Spirit.

Do we realize this as much as we should? Any assembly or church
of the living God (and I use this in the strictest New Testament
sense, a company of called-out believers) is the habitation of God
through the Spirit. That is why the church should be kept holy; that
is why unsaved people should have no part in its fellowship, be-

cause they are not members of the true church. That is why Christians who are members of that church should be careful to avoid all worldliness and everything that would dishonor the Lord Jesus Christ. May God move us to live in such a way that we will glorify His name in this world.

EPHESIANS 3

The Revelation of the Mystery (3:1-13)

In Ephesians 3 the apostle unfolded the great secret that had been in the heart of God from eternity. In a very special sense Paul was the chosen one to make known this mystery in all its fullness. On the other hand we need to guard against the idea that no others participated in this knowledge, for in verse 5 of Ephesians 3 he declared, "It is now revealed unto his holy apostles and prophets by the Spirit." Others, therefore, shared with him in this blessed knowledge, but preeminently he was the apostle used by God to reveal the mystery.

No one else wrote of the body of Christ, among all the New Testament writers. This teaching came first to Paul that he might communicate it to others. But the truth that Jew and Gentile were to be blessed in the same way on the basis of pure grace was made known to the twelve. Our Lord taught this truth. "His own sheep" from the Jewish fold, and "other sheep" of the Gentiles were to form "one flock" under the fostering care of "one Shepherd" (John 10:4,16). Peter's vision of the sheet let down from Heaven revealed the same glorious mystery. But the revelation of the one body was the special truth committed to Paul and given to him in seed form at the very time of his conversion, as the words, "Why persecutest thou me?" imply (Acts 9:4). Christ's question to Paul indicated that to touch a saint on earth was to touch the Head in Heaven. Thus was Paul taught the unity of the body and its union with the glorified Head.

We might say it was because of this very truth that he was in prison at the time he wrote the Ephesian letter. I think this is indicated by the expression "I, Paul, the prisoner of Jesus Christ for you Gentiles." You will remember that in his defense on the temple stairs at Jerusalem, he announced that he had been commanded by the Lord to go to the Gentiles. The anger of his Jewish hearers was stirred to the depths, and they cried, "Away with such a fellow from the earth: for it is not fit that he should live" (Acts 22:22). We, therefore, who are Gentiles have special reason to be grateful to Paul for his faithfulness in proclaiming God's purpose for us in His divine program. Because of this he suffered persecution, and spent many weary months in prison rather than surrender in the least degree the truth of God committed to him.

In Ephesians 3, as in Colossians, he indicated that his was a double ministry. First, he spoke "of the dispensation of the grace of God" which was given him (2). A dispensation is a stewardship. Paul, like every true New Testament preacher, was a steward of the grace of God. Notice how the apostle Peter also wrote: "As every man has received the gift, even so minister the same one to another, as good stewards of the manifold grace of God" (1 Peter 4:10). Grace, we have already observed, is God's unmerited favor to those who have deserved the very opposite. It is this grace that is proclaimed in the gospel. And this, of course, is the first part of the mystery. The apostle goes on to show that he was not only a minister of the gospel, but in a special sense a minister of this now revealed secret.

He said that by revelation the mystery was made known to him, and he called it the "mystery of Christ." It is God's wonderful secret concerning the glory of His blessed Son. How good it is to know that Christ's glory and our salvation are eternally linked and can never be separated. Speaking of the mystery he said, "As I wrote afore in few words" (3). This, I take it, refers to what he had already said in chapter 1:9-13. He will now elaborate that more fully. He had also written before to others concerning this mystery (See Romans 16:25-26; 1 Corinthians 2:7, and other Pauline Epistles). I mention this because of the unwarranted position taken by some that the mystery was never revealed until Paul's imprisonment. On the contrary, he had been proclaiming it from the very beginning, both by voice and pen.

Now what is this mystery that in other ages was hidden from the sons of men? We are told in verse 6: "That the Gentiles should be fellowheirs, and of the same body, and partakers of his promise in Christ by the gospel." How does this differ from the Old Testament declaration that God would bless the Gentiles through Israel? The great difference is this: According to the Old Testament prophets the day is coming when Israel will be restored to covenant relationship with God and will be brought into a place of special blessing here on the earth. The Gentile nations living at that time will be blessed with and in subjection to them. But the great truth for our age is that God is now calling out a people for Himself to be the body and bride of His Son throughout the ages to come. Through those called-out people He will administer the affairs of a redeemed universe. This group is composed of both Jews and Gentiles who have been born again and united to the Lord Himself by the Spirit, thus becoming one body with Him and each other. It was this great truth that Paul was specially called to minister "according to the gift of the grace of God," which had been given to him. The Holy Spirit effectively worked in and through him to bring lost sinners of the Gentiles into this wonderful place of privilege and inalienable blessing.

Note how meekly the apostle spoke of himself, even in connection with this great ministry committed to him, which was enough to have turned any ordinary man's head. He said, "Unto me, who am less than the least of all saints, is this grace given." He did not boast of the abundance of the revelation made known to him, but accepted it as a divine trust that he was to minister for the glory of God and the blessing of others. What a different spirit often motivates some today, who, getting a little smattering of truth, are carried away by their fancied superior intelligence. They exhibit the most shocking pride and conceit because of the imagined inferiority of other believers who have not yet attained to their knowledge of the truth! Surely every new divine truth given to us should only humble us the more as we realize that we have nothing that we have not received. Apart from divine grace, we would still be in our natural darkness and ignorance. Paul took a very humble position as he went about preaching among the Gentiles the unsearchable riches of Christ. To those who were in the greatest spiritual poverty he eloquently proclaimed the availability of inexpressible wealth. Paul wanted all men to enjoy the blessings and reality of the fellowship of this mystery. Men form their secret societies and delight to meet in hidden places to enjoy together mysteries that others cannot share. The Christian is through grace already a member of the society of the redeemed, a fellowship divinely formed by the indwelling of the Holy Spirit. And as a member of that society he can enjoy with fellow believers the marvelous secret that God has now made known.

From the beginning of the world this mystery was hidden in God "who created all things by Jesus Christ" (9). Observe, it was not simply hidden in the Bible, as though the Old Testament contained this message and we only needed to ferret it out. But it was hidden in God, and could not have been understood by man until it was made known by divine revelation. When the Lord Jesus Christ was rejected by Israel, and the Holy Spirit descended to bear witness to the perfection of Christ's finished work, it pleased God to make known this mystery. Even angels, whether good or bad, had no knowledge of it until it was given to God's saints on earth. This, I understand, is the meaning of the remarkable statement of verse 10, "To the intent that now unto the principalities and powers in heavenly places might be known [through] the church, the manifold wisdom of God." That is, the unseen hosts of glorious beings in Heaven, as well as the vast armies of fallen spirits dominated by Satan, are learning the many-sided wisdom of God. As they observe what God is doing here on earth in His church they are learning, "the purpose [of the ages] which he purposed in Christ Jesus our Lord." One of our poets has written: "Through the ages / One unceasing purpose runs."

The humble student of the Word of God can see unfolded in the New Testament the great purpose that God had in mind. He created the universe and man and counseled with Himself to take out of that world from the children of Adam a vast company who would be united to His blessed Son throughout eternity. All will work out for the glory of Christ Jesus, our Lord.

In Him we now have immediate access with fullest confidence into the presence of God (12). We are so intimately linked up with

Him, so truly one with Him, that we can approach the throne of grace without dread or fear, knowing that all we ask in His name or by His authority, the Father delights to do.

No wonder the apostle could glory in suffering because of this great truth. He would not have the saints become discouraged because of His trials, but rather he would have them remember that whatever tribulation he was passing through was on their behalf and for their glory (13).

The extent to which we accept these precious truths for ourselves, will determine our practical sanctification. The Christian who truly understands his unity with Christ, and therefore with all who are in Christ, cannot be sectarian in heart or practice, but must embrace all believers in his fellowship and interest.

To profess to believe the truth of the one body is one thing. To be governed by this belief is quite another. So intimate is the link that binds all believers to each other and to our glorified Head in Heaven that everything I say or do as a Christian has an effect for good or ill on all my fellow members, just as every part of the human body affects every other part. This amazing truth should make us very careful in our walk and our attitude toward one another.

Paul's Second Prayer for the Saints (3:14-21)

In the first chapter of this precious Epistle we have Paul's prayer for knowledge, and in the third, his prayer for love. After reading the first prayer we naturally find ourselves looking out over the great sphere of God's eternal purpose, trying to take in the scope of His wonderful pre-arranged divine plan. But, as we read the second prayer and meditate on it, we find ourselves looking up in adoring gratitude, with our hearts going out in love to the One who first loved us.

We read in verse 14, "For this cause I bow my knees unto the Father of our Lord Jesus Christ." "For this cause"—For what cause? What motivated Paul to pray for these people? It was his deep interest in the people of God. He desired that they should fully experience their privileges in Christ and understand the great mystery of which he had spoken.

The expression, "I bow my knees," is a very beautiful one and suggests intensity of feeling. Have you ever noticed that if you are just quietly engaged in prayer or meditation, you may sit, perhaps as I often do, in a comfortable big chair with your open Bible before you, and as one thought or another comes, you close your eyes and lift your heart to God in prayer? Or when you come together with God's people, you love to stand in holy silence before God, joining with someone who is leading in prayer. But when you are intensely in earnest, when something has fairly gripped you that stirs you to deepest supplication, you find yourself almost irresistibly forced to your knees.

"I bow my knees unto the Father of our Lord Jesus Christ." We noticed that the first prayer is addressed to the God of our Lord Jesus Christ, for God is the source of all knowledge. But this second prayer, which has to do more with family relationship, is addressed to the Father of our Lord Jesus Christ. Divine titles are used most discriminately in the Word of God; never in the careless way that we so often use them. We might not think it made any difference whether one said, "I address myself to the *God* of our Lord Jesus," or, "I bow my knees to the *Father* of our Lord Jesus," but it made a great deal of difference to the apostle. It indicated the different thoughts that were in his mind. When I think of God, I think of the maker of all things, the planner of all things who fitted the ages together. But I think of the Father as the One from whose bosom the eternal Son came into this world, becoming man for our salvation. Before He left this world Jesus said to Mary, "I ascend unto my Father, and your Father; and to my God, and your God" (John 20:17). There you have the two thoughts: God, the source of all counsels; the Father, the source of all family affections—the very center of family relationship.

"The Father...Of whom the whole family in heaven and earth is named." "The whole family" is undoubtedly a correct rendering here, and yet "every family" would be just as correct. "The whole family," however, conveys the most precious thought. This phrase means that all saints in earth and Heaven constitute one great family of born-again ones, of whom God is the father. But I am thinking too of the great hosts of angels never redeemed by the blood of

Christ because they have never fallen; even those who fell found no Savior. The angels also acknowledge the fatherhood of God, but they are servants, waiting on the family. Then there is the family of the Old Testament saints. There was the antediluvian family, the patriarchal family, the Israelites, those who were truly of Israel. All these were families through the past dispensations. Today there is the church of this age of grace, and in the future there will be the glorious kingdom family. There are dispensational distinctions, but all receive life from the same blessed Person, and all together adore and worship Him. Notice that the whole family is located in Heaven and on earth. Those who are dead to us are alive to God above.

As we try to understand this prayer I want you to think of seven words that I believe will help us to grasp its scope. First, there is our *endowment*. "That he would grant you, according to the riches of his glory." You may come to God in prayer for anything, and realize that since you have such a marvelous endowment from which to draw, you do not need to fear to present your petitions to God. You cannot ask too much. We are reminded of the man who came to a king asking for something, and the king gave to him out of his abundant treasure until the man said, "Your majesty, that is too much! That is too much!" The king smiled and said, "It may seem too much for you to take, but it is not too much for me to give." And so our blessed God gives out of His abundance.

He is "able to do exceeding abundantly above all that we ask or think." He does not say, as we sometimes suppose, "Able to do exceeding abundantly above all that we *can* ask or think," for we might be like little children asking for the moon. But Paul said that God does for us, "exceeding abundantly above all that we ask or think." When we come to Him in the name of Jesus, bringing our petitions, there is more in that great endowment fund than we can ever exhaust.

"According to the riches of his glory." "According to," not "out of the riches of His glory." We have noticed the difference between these two expressions when commenting on a similar passage found in Ephesians 1:7, so we need not repeat the illustration used then. But it means much to the soul when one truly sees this distinction.

Next Paul prayed that the Ephesians "be strengthened with might by his Spirit in the inner man." This speaks of our *enduement* or empowerment. Do you sometimes feel your limitations, your weakness, your lack of purpose, your powerlessness when it comes to living for God and witnessing for Him? Do you feel as though you might as well give up for the little you accomplish? Do you say, "If I only had more strength, how different it might be"? Listen! The excellency of the power is of God, not of us, and the Holy Spirit who dwells within us is ready to work in and through us to the glory of our Lord Jesus Christ. So the prayer is that we may be "strengthened with might by his Spirit in the inner man." Some people have an idea that a Christian is a walking storage battery. You hear people pray, "O God, give me more power, fill me with power." The idea they have is that the old battery is pretty well run down. "Put another one in, Lord," is what they seem to say. No, you are not a storage battery; you are in connection with the great eternal dynamo, and the Holy Spirit works in and through you to the glory of the Lord Jesus Christ as you yield yourself to Him. He Himself is the source of all power, and that power is to be used by the people of God.

"That Christ may dwell in your hearts by faith." The next word is *enthronement*. It is Christ sitting on the throne of our hearts dominating, controlling us for the glory of God, His blessed pierced hands guiding and directing everything. It is not Christ received as an occasional visitor, not Christ recognized merely as a guest, but Christ abiding within as our living, loving Lord: Christ dwelling in the heart by faith. You remember the saying, "If Christ is not Lord of all, He is not Lord at all." He does not want second place. He must be first if your life is going to be that which it should.

"That ye, being rooted and grounded in love." This phrase suggests our *establishment*. *Rooted* and *grounded* are two very different terms. When I was a boy, the schoolteacher used to tell me that I must not mix my metaphors. For instance, I should not start with the figure of a ship and change to that of a railroad in the same sentence. But the Holy Ghost is wonderfully independent in His use of metaphors. He speaks of being rooted like a tree, and grounded like a building that is raised on a great foundation. Rooted and grounded in what? In love. What is love? It is the great rock foundation on which we build, for God is love. He who is rooted in love is rooted in God, and therefore, "the righteous shall flourish like the palm tree: he shall grow like a cedar in Lebanon" (Psalm 92:12). The believer is like the trees, for they draw their nourishment from the living God Himself. Great Christian character will be established when one is founded on this Rock, building on God Himself, "rooted and grounded in love"!

"That ye...May be able to comprehend with all saints." This speaks of our *enlightenment*. Individually, you will never be able to completely understand God's purposes in grace. But you comprehend a little, and another Christian a little, and I a little, and with all the saints together we begin to get some idea of God's wonderful purpose of grace. Therefore, we need one another; we need fellowship; we need to be helpers of each other's faith. The feeblest, weakest member of the body of Christ is necessary, for God may give understanding to some weak brother that some strong active Christian may never get at all. Paul prayed that we be enabled "to comprehend with all saints what is the breadth, and length, and depth, and height." Of what? Some say love. But previously in the chapter he had been speaking about God's wonderful purpose of the ages, God's great plan. Paul was praying that by the Spirit you may be able to comprehend with all saints what is the breadth, and length, and depth, and height of the vast system of grace that God is working out through the ages of time, and which will be consummated in the ages to come.

In school I was told that no solid could have more than three dimensions—length, breadth, and thickness. But we have here length, breadth, depth, and height—four dimensions. Could you draw a picture of this? Could you draw an illustration of length, breadth, depth, and height? How would you do it? Some of the old Greek philosophers used to reason about a possible fourth dimension, and with them it was a kind of weird spiritual dimension. That is not such a bad idea. When Napoleon's soldiers opened the prison of the Inquisition, in an underground dungeon they found the skeleton of a prisoner. The flesh and clothing had long since gone, but the remnants of an ankle bone with a chain attached to it were still there. On the wall they saw cut into the rock with a sharp piece of metal a cross. Above the cross in Spanish was the word for *height*, and below it the word for *depth*, and on one arm the word for *length*, and on the other the word for *breadth*. As that poor prisoner of so long ago was starving to death, his soul was contemplating the wonder of God's purpose of grace, and to Him the figure of the cross summed it all up—the length, the breadth, the depth, the height!

Next Paul prayed that we may "know the love of Christ, which passeth knowledge." Surely this is our *enlargement*. We glory as we comprehend the knowledge of the love of Christ. But what a strange expression is Paul's petition! He prayed that we may know the unknowable: "The love of Christ, which passeth knowledge." See that darling little baby in the mother's arms, looking up and cooing and responding to the mother's smile? You or I might say, "May I hold the baby?" and hold out our hands, and he would look at us and cling the more tightly to the mother. If we insist on taking him, he might utter a piercing cry that would say, "I do not know you; I do not know whether you love babies or not, but I know my mother's love and can trust her." And yet, what does the baby really know of the love of a mother? What does he understand about the reasons behind a mother's love? But he enjoys it nevertheless. And so the youngest saint in Christ knows the love of the Savior, and the most mature saint is seeking to know in greater fullness that love that passeth knowledge.

> Oh, the love of Christ is boundless,
> Broad and long and deep and high!
> Every doubt and fear is groundless,
> Now the Word of faith is nigh.
> Jesus Christ for our salvation,
> Came and shed His precious blood;
> Clear we stand from condemnation,
> In the risen Son of God.

Then notice the last point in Paul's prayer, "That ye might be filled [unto] all the fulness of God" (19). This is our *enrichment*. The King James version, "Filled with all the fulness of God," is not totally accurate for you could not hold all the fullness of God.

Solomon said, "Behold the heaven of heavens cannot contain thee" (1 Kings 8:27). Yet we read that He dwells in the heart of him that is humble and contrite. Walking by the seaside one time, someone touched on the real meaning of this word. He picked up one of the beautiful seashells and put it down in the sand where the water had ebbed for a moment or two. Then as they watched, the sea came rolling in and the shell was filled, and he said, "See! Filled unto all the fullness of the ocean." So you and I as we live in fellowship with God may be filled unto His fullness. We are in Him and He is in us, and thus Paul's prayer is answered.

And now notice the closing wonderful benediction of Paul's prayer: "Now unto him that is able to do exceeding abundantly above all that we ask or think." Does it say "Now unto him that is able to do *above* all we ask"? No, that is not enough. Is it, "Able to do *abundantly above* all that we ask"? That is not enough. Is it, "Able to do *exceeding abundantly above* all that we ask?" No, still that does not reach the limit. "Unto him that is able to do *exceeding abundantly above all that we ask or think.*" You need not fear to come to God about anything.

Are you troubled about present circumstances? Have you availed yourself of the abundant resources of God? If your heart is right with God and you come to Him and make effective use of the power He has for you, you can be sure of a wonderful answer. "According to the power that worketh in us"—this is the divine energy that works through poor feeble creatures such as we are. "Unto him be glory in the church by Christ Jesus throughout all ages, world without end. Amen." He is the One in whom God will find His pleasure throughout all eternity.

EPHESIANS 4

The Walk Worthy of Our Calling (4:1-6)

In chapters one to three we have been studying the doctrinal section of this letter to the Ephesians. We now take up the practical part, that which has to do with our lives as those who have been made members of Christ's body through grace. Notice how tenderly the apostle wrote: "I therefore, the prisoner of the Lord, beseech you that ye walk worthy of the vocation wherewith ye are called."

Wherever grace rules in the soul, "I command" is changed to "I beseech." You do not find the apostle lording his position over the faith of the people of God, but graciously, tenderly pleading with them, rather than sternly ordering their behavior. He spoke of himself in a way that certainly must have touched the heart of everyone who read this letter in its original setting. The Ephesians had come to know the Savior's love through Paul, and the link between a preacher and those who have been brought to Christ as a result of his ministry is a very real one. Hearts are very closely bound together when they stand in that relationship. What must they have felt when they realized that the man of God to whom they owed so much was lying in a Roman prison, and he was there not because of any ill-doing on his part, but because of his faithful proclamation of the gospel that meant so much to them? He was a prisoner of the Lord, and from his prison cell he wrote this letter, beseeching them to walk worthy of the vocation wherewith they were called.

Our vocation is, of course, our calling. Paul referred to that which he had written before—the blessedness of the new life. In view of the fact that I have been redeemed to God by the precious blood of Christ; in view of the fact that I am a member now of His body, of His flesh, and of His bones; in view of the fact that I am a living stone built into that temple of God by the Holy Spirit, that temple in which He dwells, my behavior is to be ordered by God. I am to walk worthy of the calling I have received. Elsewhere we are told to walk worthy of God and of the Lord (see Colossians 1:10 and 1 Thessalonians 2:12).

"With all lowliness and meekness, with longsuffering, forbearing one another in love." I spent quite a little time over this verse. Every expression in it was a challenge to me, and I kept asking myself the question, "To what extent have I risen to the standard that is set here? I must present this to others as the divine standard for a Christian's behavior. To what extent am I measuring up to it?" And the more I carefully examined every expression both in the English and in the original Greek, the more humiliated and ashamed before God I was as I realized how far short I have come from living out what we have here. Every word is important.

"With all lowliness." That word is found only once elsewhere in the New Testament and that is in Philippians 2:3: "Let nothing be done through strife or vainglory; but in lowliness of mind let each esteem other better than themselves." The original word means "modesty," that is, an utter lack of self-assertiveness. Pride is so characteristic of us as fallen creatures. We who have nothing to be proud of are sometimes proud of our very crudity and ignorance.

A young minister arose in a conference and said, "I am against education. I don't believe in education. I read no books except the Bible; I don't profess to know nothing about literature or anything of that kind; I am just an ignorant man. But the Lord has taken me up, and is using me, and I am not at all interested in schools, or colleges or education. I am proud to be just what I am." An old preacher arose and said, "Do I understand that our dear young brother is proud of his ignorance? If so, all I have to say is that he has a great deal to be proud of." Most of us are that way; we are proud of the very thing of which we ought to be ashamed. We boast of our accomplishments and ability, even as children. One of the first things parents must learn in training their children is to curb that natural tendency to boastfulness. But as Christians, how completely we should be delivered from this. We have nothing that we have not received. Every blessing we have we owe to divine grace. With what modesty, then, should we behave ourselves!

The word *meekness* is found a number of times in the New Testament and it is used of our Lord Himself. The apostle said, "We beseech you by the meekness and gentleness of Christ" (2 Corinthians 10:1), and Christ said, "Take my yoke upon you, and learn of me; for I am meek and lowly in heart: and ye shall find rest unto your souls" (Matthew 11:29). The root of the original word really means "humility," a spirit that never takes personal offense. Somebody says something unkind about me. I flare up in a moment. Why? Because I am not meek. In Mark 15 we read that "the chief priests accused [Jesus] of many things: but he answered nothing." "When he was reviled, reviled not again; when he suffered, he threatened not" (1 Peter 2:23). That is meekness.

The next word Paul used is *longsuffering*. This is a favorite word of the apostle, and we also find it used three times by the apostle Peter. It means literally, "to endure with unruffled temper." Do you know very much about longsuffering? "Well," you say, "I would not mind if what was said about me had been true, but when I know it isn't true, I can't stand it." Therefore, the need of longsuffering. It is the flesh that talks like that, not the new nature but the old. Many years ago I had a friend whose name was George. Sometimes he would fly off and lose his temper. But he was always brought back to earth when someone looked at him quietly and said, "Is that old George or new George talking?" In a moment the tears would come. Even now, though he has been gone thirty years, I can hear him say, "That's old George; new George would never behave that way. I must punish that old George. He has no right to behave like that." Yes, the old nature is quick to take offense, quick to flare up if not properly appreciated, but the new nature just bows in meekness and lets the waves and billows pass over and is undisturbed by them.

The last word to consider in this verse is *forbearing*: "Forbearing one another in love." This word occurs in only one other book of the New Testament and that is in Colossians 3:13: "Forbearing one another, and forgiving one another, if any man have a quarrel against any: even as Christ forgave you, so also do ye." Literally, *forbearance* means "to put up with."

Now taking all that into account I thought I would try to translate Ephesians 4:2 myself: "With all modesty and humbleness of spirit, with unruffled temper, lovingly putting up with all that is disagreeable in other people." That is a literal rendering of the original. That describes the Spirit of Christ. As we meditate on it and think of all that is involved in it, how can we do other than hang our heads in shame and confess that in many things we offend. May we be so yielded to the control of the Holy Spirit of God that this Christlike character may indeed become real in our lives.

The apostle continued, "Endeavoring to keep the unity of the Spirit in the bond of peace" (3). Others have translated it, "Giving diligence to keep the unity of the Spirit in the bond of peace." Observe, he does not say, "Giving diligence to keep *the unity of the body*." We do not have anything to do with preserving the unity of the body. God is looking after that. He binds believers together in Christ, gives His Holy Spirit to dwell within, and links them one to another, and to their glorious Head in Heaven. The body of Christ is always complete as God looks at it.

People talk about heartless divisions that tear apart the body of Christ, but these divisions do not tear apart the body of Christ. The body of Christ is not composed of all the different sects and denominations. If you were to gather all the different Catholic sects together, all the different eastern orthodox sects together and all the Protestant sects together and unite them all in one big church, that would not be the body of Christ. That would contain a great many people who are in the body of Christ but it would also include a great many who are not. On the other hand, after you had gathered all these denominations together, there would still be a great many outside that would be members of the body of Christ. The church, which is His body, and the church, which some call the visible body of Christ, are not the same thing. The body of Christ consists only of those who are regenerated and born again by the Holy Spirit and joined to Christ in glory by the Spirit's baptism. All the divisions in Christendom cannot split that body. But what have these various denominations done? They certainly have denied the unity of the Spirit. The apostle would have us recognize this unity that God Himself established, and so he said, "Endeavoring to keep the unity of the Spirit in the bond of peace."

The Spirit unites us to the body that He has formed, and now He says, "I want you to recognize it." When you meet with fellow believers, do you endeavor to keep the unity of the Spirit, do you realize that you belong to them and they belong to you? "But," you say, "they do not see things the way I do." If they belong to Christ, they belong to you and you to them. We are to accept them in the uniting bond of peace.

Some years ago I was taken ill in the midst of a series of meetings at Minneapolis. After my fourth address I went out one Sunday noon to take dinner, and right after the meal I collapsed. When I regained consciousness I had a fever of one hundred and two degrees and was ill with typhoid. I was down for six weeks. As soon as I had strength enough to start home my friends helped me get to the train station. The porter on the train was very courteous. He made up a berth and put both mattresses on, and let me recline there all day long.

The first morning as I lay there with a lot of pillows behind me, I took out my Bible. (Of course you never start the day without at least a little portion from the Word of God; do you? You do? Well that is why you have so many bad days.) I was reading from the Word of God when a German lady came walking by, and she stopped and asked with a pronounced German accent, "What's that? A Bible?" I said, "Yes." "Well, you have your morning worship all by yourself? Wait," she said, "I go get my Bible and we have it together." She came back and settled herself on my couch and said, "Where are you reading?" A little later a tall gentleman came by, and stopped and in a Scandinavian accent asked, "Reading the Bible? Well, I think I'll go get mine, too." He came back with his Bible, and in a few minutes I was amazed at the people who crowded around.

They did the same thing every day, and we had a delightful time all the way to California. I would get my Bible, and then they would begin to come, and sometimes there would be as many as twenty-eight people with their Bibles. The conductor would go all through the cars and say, "The camp meeting is beginning in car number so-and-so. Any wanting to take advantage are invited." Sometimes they would start a hymn; sometimes we would have a little prayer; and sometimes it would be only the Bible reading, and they would ask questions.

That fellowship continued until we reached Sacramento, where some of the cars were separated to go down the valley. So the people from the other cars came in to say goodbye, and this dear German sister came and said, "Oh, it has been just like a camp meeting all the way. It has fed my soul. I am going to Turlock, but I want to ask you, What denomination are you?" "Well," I said, "I belong to the same denomination that David did." "What was that? I didn't know that David belonged to any," she asked. "David said, 'I am a companion of all them that fear Thee and keep Thy precepts,'" I answered. "Yah, yah," she said; "that is a good church to belong to."

I suppose if we had questioned those people, we would have found that we belonged to a dozen different sects. But we found we were all one in Christ. Oh, that we might endeavor "to keep the unity of the Spirit in the bond of peace," not in contentiousness, not in quarreling, but all alike seeking to glorify the Lord Jesus Christ, our Savior.

In verses 4-6 of Ephesians 4 the apostle brings before us a sevenfold unity. Notice, "There is one body, and one Spirit, even as ye are called in one hope of your calling; One Lord, one faith, one baptism, One God and Father of all, who is above all, and through all, and in you all." Seven different unities all linked up in one. These verses comprise one great confession, and yet it is easy to see that there are three distinct spheres indicated, becoming larger and larger. Verse 4 speaks of that unity which is absolutely vital, "There is one body." That is the body of Christ, and as we have seen, that body is composed only of people who have been washed from their sins in the blood of our Lord Jesus Christ. They have been regenerated by the Word and by the Spirit, and thus made members of Christ. Then in the second place, "There is one Spirit," and this is the one Holy Spirit by whose operation we have been baptized into the body of Christ. We read in 1 Corinthians 12:13, "For by one

Spirit are we all baptized into one body, whether we be Jews or
Gentiles, whether we be bond or free; and have been all made to
drink into one Spirit." Third, we are given one hope—"Even as ye
are called in one hope of your calling." All believers have the same
blessed hope, the hope of some day, some day soon, beholding the
face of our Lord Jesus Christ and being transformed into His image.
All real believers are included in this first sphere—one body, one
Spirit, one hope of your calling.

But now the second sphere is a little bit wider. It does not necessarily include only those who are born again. It may include those
who have made a profession that is not real. "One Lord, one faith,
one baptism." You see, there are those who say, "Lord, Lord," who
have never been born again. Jesus says that in the day of judgment
many will come to Him and say, "Lord, Lord, have we not proph-
esied in thy name? and in thy name have cast out devils? and in thy
name done many wonderful works? And then will I profess unto
them, I never knew you: depart from me, ye that work iniquity"
(Matthew 7:22-23). Take, for instance, that part of the world which
we call "Christendom." What do people write at the head of their
letters? They write 1936 (this sermon was delivered in 1936). And
what does that mean? It means, in the year of our lord 1936. I suppose every racketeer and gangster in Chicago dates his letters that
way. "Why call ye me, Lord, Lord, and do not the things which I
say?" (Luke 6:46) There are lots of hypocrites in Christendom who
call Him Lord, and yet show by their lives that they have never
been born again.

Also in the second sphere is the one faith. This is not the faith by
which we are saved, but the faith of the Christian church, "the faith
which was once delivered unto the saints" (Jude 3). It is the one
standard of truth that God has given to be proclaimed in the world,
it is that which the apostle calls *the faith*. Faith in Christ is a personal confidence in Jesus, but *the faith* is the body of Christian doctrine.

Then there is baptism, the outward expression of allegiance to
Christ. Some ask, "Do you think that baptism here is water baptism,
or the baptism of the Spirit?" I say without a moment's hesitation,
"water baptism," for we have seven unities. We have already had

the baptism of the Spirit—"one body, one Spirit"—and we do not have the Spirit repeated here. If it were the baptism of the Spirit, you would have only a sixfold unity, but water baptism is the outward expression of allegiance to Christ. A man may profess to belong to Christ and be baptized, but that does not prove he is really born again. The mark of Christ has been put on some people and yet they have never truly received Him into their hearts. What a solemn thing this is! I wonder if any of you are in the wider circle. You have never been born again, you are not in the first circle but are among those who have made an insincere profession, therefore you are in the second circle. Can it be that the mark of Christ has been placed on you—that you have been baptized in the name of the Father and of the Son and of the Holy Ghost—and yet you have never trusted Christ? What an awful thing for a lost one in the pit of eternal damnation to have to say, "I bore Christ's mark on earth; I was baptized in recognition of His death and suffering, and yet here I am lost for all eternity because I did not trust that Savior who suffered for me."

Notice the third circle. This is very much wider than the others, for it takes in God's relationship to the entire creation. "One God," and as such He is in relationship to all His creatures. "And Father of all, who is above all, and through all, and in you all." This is not the modern doctrine of the universal fatherhood of God and the universal brotherhood of man, but it means that God is the Creator of all men. He is a distinct personality. This is not pantheism, not God as a principle, but God, a divine personality, and yet immanent in grace, not far from any one of us.

He is the living, transcendent God over all, pre-eminent, directing all things, pervading everything. He is "in you all." That is the distinction between God's attitude toward the world as a whole and toward those who have been born again—"in you all." If you have accepted Christ, if you have trusted Him, God dwells in you. What a marvelous truth this is! He said, "I will dwell in them, and walk in them" (2 Corinthians 6:16). As we walk in this world we can realize that God is walking with us, and so we may well come back to the exhortation with which we began: "Walk worthy of the vocation wherewith ye are called."

Gifts from the Ascended Christ (4:7-13)

Our attention in these verses is especially drawn to the gifts that the ascended Christ has given His church for its upbuilding. First observe that there are gifts for all—"Unto every one of us is given grace according to the measure of the gift of Christ." Certain gifts are more outstanding and visible, but every member of the body of Christ has something that he may contribute to the blessing of the whole. No matter how feeble, how insignificant, how relatively unknown he may be, he has received something from the risen Lord for the help of all the rest.

Many parts of our physical bodies are unseen and function without any outward evidence of their working. Yet they are very important in connection with the healthy growing and maintaining of the body. In the same way every believer has his place to fill in the body of Christ. If he is not functioning according to the will of God, in some respect he affects the whole body negatively; but if he is using his gifts according to the will of God, he affects the entire body of Christ for good. These gifts come from the ascended Lord.

Verse 8 is quoted from Psalm 68: "Thou hast ascended on high, thou hast led captivity captive." Just what is meant by that rather peculiar expression? It is a Hebraism, taken over literally from the Hebrew. Psalm 68:18 reads: "Thou hast ascended on high, thou hast led captivity captive: thou hast received gifts for men: yea, for the rebellious also, that the Lord God might dwell among them." Some scholars attempt to explain this expression, "captivity captive," by translating it "a multitude of captives." But when we realize that this is simply a translation of an expression in the Psalm, we have to inquire whether the Hebrew text could be translated, "A multitude of captives." I think any Hebrew scholar would acknowledge that it could not. And that is not the only place where this expression is found.

In Judges 5 we read the same expression. Deborah is praising the Lord for the great victory over Canaan. In verse 12 we read, "Awake, awake, Deborah: awake, utter a song: arise, Barak, and lead thy captivity captive, thou son of Abinoam." What does the expression mean there? It could only mean one thing—"Lead captive him who held you captive." That seems to be the meaning of Psalm 68:18, and also of this quotation in the Epistle to the Ephesians.

In Isaiah 14 we have a similar expression that would adequately interpret "captivity captive." We read, "And the people shall take them, and bring them to their place: and the house of Israel shall possess them in the land of the Lord for servants and handmaids: and they shall take them captives, whose captives they were; and they shall rule over their oppressors" (Isaiah 14:2). This surely makes the meaning clear. In our present passage the teaching is this, that our Lord in His triumph over death led captive him who had the power of death up to that time, that He might deliver those "who through fear of death were all their lifetime subject to bondage" (Hebrews 2:15). In other words, our mighty enemy, Satan, is now a conquered foe. He has been led captive at the chariot wheels of Christ, and our Lord has now ascended as man and taken His place on the throne of the Majesty in Heaven. There from His exalted seat in glory He gives these gifts to His church for its edification and blessing.

"Now that he ascended, what is it but that he also descended first into the lower parts of the earth? He that descended is the same also that ascended up far above all heavens, that he might fill all things." We are reminded that He who has gone up higher than any other man ever went, once for our redemption went down lower than any other man has gone. I wonder if our souls really take in the fact that He is a man like ourselves, only glorified, sinless, and holy, sitting today on the throne of God. A man's heart beats in His breast, and there are no sorrows that come to His people but what He enters sympathetically, compassionately, into them. Therefore, having "not an high priest which cannot be touched with the feeling of our infirmities, but was in all points tempted like as we are," we may "come boldly unto the throne of grace, that we may obtain mercy, and find grace to help in time of need" (Hebrews 4:15-16).

There's a Man in the glory I know very well,
I have known Him for years, and His goodness can tell;
One day in His mercy He knocked at my door,
And asking admittance knocked many times o'er.

But when I went to Him and stood face to face
And listened a while to His story of grace,
How He suffered for sinners and put away sin,
I heartily, thankfully, welcomed Him in.

And now I have the assurance from the Word of God that that Man sits there at the Father's right hand, ever living to make intercession for His needy people as they go through this world. Go to Him in the hour of trial, "tell not half the story, but the whole," and be assured that He will listen sympathetically and undertake for you according to the riches of His grace. He always has taken it upon Himself to work for His people in a marvelous way.

"He gave some, apostles; and some, prophets; and some, evangelists; and some, pastors and teachers; For the perfecting of the saints, for the work of the ministry, for the edifying of the body of Christ." These are the gifts that Christ Himself has given. In 1 Corinthians 12 Paul listed various operations of the Holy Spirit through the church in the beginning of its early conflict with heathenism and Judaism. But in Ephesians the gifts are for the building and maintaining of the church. They were given by the risen Christ to enable the church to carry the message to a lost world, and to build up its individual members in the knowledge of Christ.

Our Lord chose apostles when He was here on earth, but said that in the glorious millennial age, they would sit on thrones judging the twelve tribes of Israel. As the ascended Christ He has given *apostles* and *prophets* to His church, but they are given from Heaven. They included the same apostles that He chose on earth, but it was after they were filled with the Holy Spirit at Pentecost that they were seen as given to the church. The apostles and prophets laid the foundation. We read in Ephesians 2:20: "And are built upon the foundation of the apostles and prophets. Jesus Christ himself being the chief corner stone." You do not lay a foundation for a building every few stories, but the foundation is built once for all and then the superstructure is erected. Long ago, nineteen hundred years ago, the apostles and prophets fulfilled their ministry. We are not looking for new apostles and prophets.

A young Mormon elder came to me at one time and asked, "What church do you belong to?" I knew at once what he had in mind, and so I replied, "I belong to the one true church that has apostles and prophets in it."

"Oh," he said, "then you must be a latter-day saint."

"No, I am a former-day saint."

"But ours is the only church that has apostles and prophets."

"I do not think so. The church that I belong to is building on the foundation of the apostles and prophets, and although they themselves have passed off the scene long ago they are still members of this church, for it does not exist only on earth. They are part of the host though they have passed from this world and are in the presence of God. They are still members of the church."

"But we have apostles and prophets in our day."

"But, you see," I said, "the apostles and prophets were to lay the foundation, and if I understand the Word of God correctly, the temple of the living God—this wonderful church He is erecting—has been building for nineteen hundred years and it is now just about completed, and you do not put a foundation on the roof. It is away down, nineteen hundred stories below, and the temple has been rising on that foundation all through the years. We are now just putting the finishing touches on the roof. We are gathering in poor sinners, just one and another here and there. They are not coming in large numbers these days, but those that are coming are being added to the roof, and it will not be long until it will be complete and then we will all go to Heaven."

The other gifts Paul listed are very obvious today. What is the *evangelist?* He is the bearer of glad tidings. The ministry of the evangelist is especially sent to the world outside of Christianity. If God gifts a man as an evangelist, He fills his heart with fervent love for a lost world and gives him the ability to proclaim the gospel in freshness and power. What a marvelous gift is that of the evangelist! We do not all have it in the way we should like to have it. It is a privilege to teach the Word and build up the saints, but when I think of the mighty men that God has qualified and sent out as evangelists to win the lost, I covet such a gift. If you are a young preacher and have the evangelistic gift, thank God for it, cherish it, do not despise it. Do not say, "I wish I could teach the Bible like certain men." It is very good if God gifts you for that, but I would rather be used of God to win lost sinners to Christ than even to teach and instruct Christians.

Someone at one time reproved Duncan Matheson for preaching the gospel at a great conference of believers, and said, "You kept all these people sitting here for an hour listening to what they already know, when they came to hear a wonderful unfolding of new truth."

"Why," he said, "were there no sinners here today?"

"Oh, there may have been a few."

"Very well, that is all right then. I did not make a mistake because if people are Christians, they will manage to wiggle awa' to Heaven some way if they never learn another thing, but poor sinners will have to be saved or be in Hell."

Never forget that. And if you are a lost sinner—Christless, hopeless—let me impress this on you: You must choose Christ or Hell, and to neglect the one is to choose the other. I wish I could proclaim that message in a way that dying men would hear, and hearing would believe and flee from the wrath to come. That is the special province of the evangelist. He goes out into the world and wins souls for Christ, and then the Spirit of God brings them into the church of God.

As we continue in Ephesians 4 we read that He also gave the gift of *pastors*. The word means "shepherds." A true pastor is a shepherd who has a heart for the sheep of Christ's flock. Our Lord challenged Peter with the words, "Lovest thou me more than these?" After Peter earnestly confessed, "Lord, thou knowest all things, thou knowest that I love thee," Jesus said, "Feed my sheep...Feed my lambs." With those words He constituted Peter a pastor of His flock. What a precious gift that is! The evangelist finds them as lost sheep wandering in the wilderness and brings them into the flock. Then the pastor seeks to lead them into the green pastures of God's Word, to minister to them when they are sick, to be with them when they are dying, to point them to the cross in the hour when faith may be weak, to enter into their sorrows: that is the work of a real pastor. No theological seminary, no college or university can make a pastor. It is the Holy Spirit of God alone who gives a man a pastor's heart, and fills him with yearning love for the people of God.

The next gift mentioned is that of the *teacher*. What is the difference between the pastor and the teacher? In 1 Corinthians 12:8 we read, "For to one is given by the Spirit the word of wisdom; to another the word of knowledge by the same Spirit." We may say that the pastor has in a peculiar sense the word of wisdom, the teacher the word of knowledge. It is the special province of the teacher to explain the truth of God's Word in a clear, orderly way so that people may grasp it and profit by it, that they may understand the divine plan and thus apply the truth to their own needs. And it is the responsibility of the pastor to press the truth home to the conscience in the power of the Holy Spirit.

Do you ever remember a time in your life when you were going through some special trial and perplexity? Perhaps you said, "I need to go to church," and you went with a heavy burden. During the meeting someone stood up to expound the Word of God, and you were edified. He took a certain portion of Scripture and made it clear and beautiful, and it did you good, but as you left the place you said, "Well, his message didn't touch my case at all. I have no more answers to my problem than I had when I came in. I am glad I came though, for I was blessed. I will always understand that portion of Scripture better than I have in the past." But you went away with the same burden with which you came. On another occasion you returned to church, and again someone read a portion of Scripture. As he began to expound it you said, "Why, he seems to know exactly what I am going through. He seems to understand exactly what my problem is. That is just what I need." And as the Word was unfolded, your soul was stirred and your heart blessed. You went away praising the Lord for giving such gifts to His people, and thanking Him that through the explanation of His Word your perplexity was removed. You were listening to the teacher in the first case, and in the second to the pastor. One had the word of knowledge and the other the word of wisdom. What is wisdom? It is knowledge applied to meeting a distinct and definite case.

Look at verse 12. Why did Christ give apostles, prophets, evangelists, pastors, and teachers? "For the perfecting of the saints, for the work of the ministry, for the edifying of the body of Christ." The punctuation in the King James version of this verse would lead us to assume that the purpose was threefold—the perfecting of the saints, the work of the ministry, and the edifying of the body of Christ. And to what would that conclusion lead you? That the work of perfecting the saints and the work of the ministry and the edifying of the body belongs entirely to those who have been set apart in a special way as pastors and teachers and evangelists. That is the conclusion many have come to, and people are quite content to depend on the man in the pulpit and say, "Don't we commission him to do the work of the ministry? Isn't he to do the work of building up the body of Christ?" But there are no punctuation marks in the original text; they have simply been put there by editors. I am going to take the liberty of removing the commas in verse 12. Go back to verse 11: "He gave some, apostles; and some, prophets; and some, evangelists; and some, pastors and teachers; For the perfecting of the saints for the work of the ministry for the edifying of the body of Christ." Do you see any difference? It is not that the pastors and teachers are a kind of close corporation whose business it is to do all these things. But when God gifts a man as a preacher or a teacher he is to exercise that gift for the developing of the saints in order that *they* might do the work of the ministry and thus build up the body of Christ. This is an altogether different thing.

A dear young fellow came to me and said, "Are any of your sermons copyrighted?"

"No, indeed they are not," I said.

"I am glad to hear it, because I heard you a week ago and went out and preached your sermon at a mission. I wondered whether I had any right to do it."

I said, "If something gripped your soul that you can pass on to somebody else and make it a blessing to them, I thank God for it. If you get a convert, you will be the father and I will be the grandfather."

I read in Moody's life story that years ago he would go on Sunday morning to hear the different preachers of the day, and then in the afternoon and evening he would be out in the missions and on the street corners preaching the sermons he had heard. He would come back and say to one of these ministers, "Doctor, I preached your sermon five times last week, and won about forty souls." The preacher would look at him in a strange way, for he had probably not seen a soul saved for weeks or months. Our risen Lord gives some the gift of apostles, some prophets, some evangelists, some pastors, and some teachers, but it is in order that all may profit thereby, for all the saints are to carry on the work of the ministry for the building up of the body of Christ. Do not be content to come to the meetings and just be a spiritual sponge. Fill up, and then let the Lord do some squeezing. Give it out to somebody else, and then you will be carrying out the true principle of New Testament ministry.

How long will this go on? "Till we all come in the unity of the faith, and of the knowledge of the Son of God, unto a perfect man, unto the measure of the stature of the fulness of Christ" (13). What does that mean? It means that this work will continue until the entire church will be gathered home to Heaven, and Christ will be fully displayed in every one of us. What is the fullness of Christ? We read in Ephesians 1:23: "the church, Which is his body, the fulness of him that filleth all in all." Christ is the Head in glory, we are the members of His body and constitute His completeness as the one new man. When at last we have gone home to Heaven, our day of toiling over, and we are in all perfection like Himself, then this kind of ministry will be ended. There will be no need for the ministry of the pastor, the teacher, or the evangelist in Heaven, for there we will all praise the name of our Lord Jesus Christ. No one will need to teach others for all will know Him from the least to the greatest.

Manifesting the Truth in Love (4:14-16)

I never knew until I became the father of children how much is involved in the words that occur in a well-known hymn, "No infant's changing pleasure / Is like my wandering mind." How children's minds jump from one thing to another! How hard it is for them to concentrate! And many of God's children are just the same. Often when one is trying to explain a truth to believers, he is embarrassed by the questions that are asked showing that his students have not been concentrating and therefore have not grasped the truth. As a result people are never truly established in the faith. It is in order to save us from this thing that God has set in His church those who are responsible to instruct and build up His saints, that they should not be like little children tossed back and forth, like leaves carried about by the wind or, using the figure the apostle had in mind, like little sailboats on the water, blown from their course and tossed by every changing wind.

Christians who are grounded in the truth of God are a blessing. But so many people always seem to be running after some new teaching, never seeming to have any discrimination. Let me give you an absurd case. Years ago as I sat in my office in Oakland there came in through the bookroom a man whose very appearance betokened a heretic. He was tall and gaunt, had long flowing hair coming down over his shoulders, and a long unkempt beard. He came up to where I sat writing. I did not want to be interrupted, for I felt that he was going to waste my time with some useless religious argument. He said, "I gather, sir, from the books I have seen in the window that you are a truth-seeker, and I thought I would come in and have a chat with you."

"You are mistaken," I said; "I am not a truth-seeker at all."

"Oh, you aren't? May I ask why you are not?"

"Why, because, sir, I have found Him who is the Way, the Truth and the Life, and therefore my seeking is at an end. Once I was a truth-seeker, but now I am a truth-finder, for I know Christ."

"Well, but are there not many things that you still need to know?"

"Oh, yes; there are a great many things that I need to know, but I have found the great Teacher, and I am not going around seeking truth any longer. He instructs me through His Word."

"Well, as for me, I am always seeking; I go anywhere and everywhere that I think I can learn more."

"Yes," I said, "I was reading of you in my Bible the other day."

"Of me?"

"Yes."

"What did it say about me?"

"It said, 'Ever learning, and never able to come to the knowledge of the truth'" (2 Timothy 3:7).

"Why, that has no reference to me," he said.

"Pardon me, but you said that you are always seeking and if a man is always seeking, he is never finding. But, you see, those of us who know Christ have found the Truth."

Then he began to tell me some of his weird gospel.

What a lot of folks there are like him in some degree, just running from one thing to another and never getting anywhere. The apostle said, "Hold fast the form of sound words" (2 Timothy 1:13), and you get sound words in the Book of God and nowhere else.

In our text we read, "That we henceforth be no more children, tossed to and fro, and carried about with every wind of doctrine, by the sleight of men and cunning craftiness, whereby they lie in wait to deceive" (Ephesians 4:14). This verse speaks of men who have selfish purposes to serve, and want to make disciples in order to profit from them. When men come to you with strange and new ideas, ask for a "Thus saith the Lord." Ask them to give chapter and verse in the Bible for the strange doctrines they bring you. If Christians would only do this, they would not be running after these modern religious fads. God's own Word has stood the test of nineteen hundred years, and you can depend on it. You can live on it and as you feed on the precious truth revealed in its pages you will grow in grace and in the knowledge of our Lord and Savior Jesus Christ.

But now, although we want to insist on a good confession, we need to also insist on a godly, Spirit-filled life. So in verse 15 we read, "But speaking the truth in love, may grow up into him in all things, which is the head, even Christ." It is an important thing to stand for the fundamentals, but as we seek to bear witness to the great fundamental truths, let us never forget that the greatest fundamental of all is love.

> Though I have the gift of prophecy, and understand all mysteries, and all knowledge; and though I have all faith, so that I could remove mountains, and have not love, I am nothing. And though I bestow all my goods to feed the poor, and though I give my body to be burned, and have not love, it profiteth me nothing (1 Corinthians 13:2-3).

It is a very interesting fact that in the original text there is only one Greek word for the three English words, *speaking the truth*. In the original it is a present participle formed from the word *truth*, and if we turn it into literal English we would have to translate it in a rather awkward way—"truthing"—"But truthing in love." Perhaps a better rendering than "speaking the truth in love," and more suited to our ears, would be "manifesting the truth in love." In other words, it is not just the testimony of the lips, declaring that certain things are divine truth, but it is the life displaying the truth. I have heard people say of certain ones, "Yes, yes; he seems to say all the right things, but I don't see much evidence of divine love in his life." And then I have heard people sometimes bear witness of others in this way: "I believe what Mr. so-and-so says because he lives it out from day to day."

A young man was asked the question, "What have you found to be the best translation of the New Testament?" Without a moment's hesitation he answered, "My mother's." His friends said, "Your mother's? I didn't know she was a scholar. Did she translate the New Testament?" The young man quickly replied, "My mother was not a scholar, she could not read a word of Greek, but she translated the New Testament into her beautiful life, and that made more of an impression on me than anything else I have ever known." That is what you and I are called to do, to manifest the truth in our lives.

We are ever to be "truthing in love." The love of God has been poured into our hearts by the Holy Spirit and we are to reveal this love in all our dealings with others. Even, "When truth compels us to contend, / What love with all our strife should blend." The Christian is never entitled to act in an un-Christlike way, no matter what the provocation. As we thus live in the power of the truth of God and are dominated by the love of Christ, we are growing up into Him, daily becoming more like Himself. Are people seeing more of Christ in you from day to day?

I remember years ago a young preacher came to the city of Toronto, where I was born and where I lived until I was ten years old. Though I was only about eight years old at the time, I recall being taken by my mother to hear this preacher, for she insisted that

I must go and hear the gospel every Sunday night. She used to say, "It is far more important that my children hear the gospel than that they have sleep, or anything else. They must know Christ from childhood up." Of course in Canada our gospel meeting used to begin at 6:30 in the evening, and children could attend and still be home and in bed in good time. Before I was ten years old I got to be quite a "sermon taster," as the Scots used to say. I loved to come home and get on a chair and imitate the preachers, trying to give the intonations of their deep Scottish voices or those from Northern Ireland, for all the preachers I heard in those days had the old country brogue.

This one particular evening I listened to a young Irish preacher— a fine, tall, handsome young man. A little group came home with us after the meeting to spend an hour or so in singing around the old-fashioned cabinet organ. Someone asked the question, "How did you like the young preacher from Ireland?" One replied, "It did me good to hear the old tongue again. It was just grand." Another said, "I thought he had a wonderful delivery; you could hear him so plainly." Another, "He seemed to me to be most eloquent." Another, "How well he knew his Bible. He opened up the truth in a beautiful way." A lady sitting quietly was asked, "And what did you think of him?" "Well, you know," she replied, "there was something about his behavior that appealed to me. He seemed the most like Jesus of any preacher I have ever listened to." How we all might wish to have that kind of recognition—to be like Jesus. Some of us, as we try to preach His Word, are made very conscious of the fact that we are so unlike Him. There is so much about us that would never have been seen in Him. Never a night goes by but that we have to bow our knees before God and acknowledge our shortcomings. But as we walk with Him, as we seek to "truth" in love, we grow up into Him, and so we become more like Him as the days go by.

It is a beautiful thing to grow old gracefully, to exhibit more of Jesus from day to day. Our blessed Head is the One from whom we draw all our supplies for spiritual upbuilding. We read, "From whom the whole body fitly joined together and compacted by that which every joint supplieth, according to the effectual working in the measure of every part, maketh increase of the body unto the edifying of itself in love" (Ephesians 4:16). Paul used the figure of the human body, and every part, every separate organ, every joint and sinew, every gland, working together for the growth of the whole body. That is the ideal picture of the Christian church and of Christian fellowship.

Have you ever read "Hebich's Tub"? It tells the story of a quaint Dutch preacher in the East Indies. Many years ago he was conducting religious services for a group of British army officers. He was characterized by a shrewd, keen humor and taught the truth by using the most amazing illustrations. He happened to know that there were certain little dissensions among the group, and so on one occasion he took for his text, "That which every joint supplieth, according to the effectual working in the measure of every part." He looked at his audience, and then with his eyes half-shut, using the illustration of a barrel, he said, "Did you effer see a tob? What iss it that makes a good tob? If you haff a good bottom to it, iss that a tob? No. If you haff a good side, iss that a tob? No. If you haff good hoops around it, iss that a good tob? No. But if you haff good boards for the bottom and fitly choined together, and then the good boards for the sides all fitly choined together, and then the good hoops and all of these things fitly choined together, you haff a tob. And it is the same with the Christian church. You haff got to haff every believer in his place, and all fitly choined together by the power of the Holy Spirit. You may haff choined the boards together, but if there iss a little pebble in between two of the staves, you do not haff a tob that will hold water. If the staves haff shrunk and drawn apart, it is useless. And if I am a Christian and haff some selfishness in me, if through selfishness or envy I do not haff real Christian fellowship, or if little things come in, I am useless. If the Colonel's lady has some unkind feeling toward the Major's lady and they come to church and join in prayer and in singing hymns and listen to the sermon, yet they are not fitly choined together, you don't have real Christian fellowship." How many little things there are that come in to hinder and keep believers from functioning as they ought!

"Fitly joined together and compacted by that which every joint supplieth." You have to contribute your share and I have to contribute mine, all for the good of the whole. And then what is the result?

"According to the effectual working in the measure of every part, maketh increase of the body unto the edifying of itself in love." May God give every one of us a deeper sense of our individual responsibility to live the truth in love for the blessing of all.

The Walk of the New Man (4:17-24)

"This I say therefore"—we may well ask, "Wherefore?" In view of all that Paul had written in the earlier part of this Epistle, he admonished his readers, "henceforth walk not as other Gentiles walk." Since, as Christians we have been chosen in Christ before the foundation of the world that we should be holy, and have been redeemed through His blood, and have been made members of His body, led by the Spirit, united to a risen Christ in glory, our lives are to be different from those around us. Christians are people called out from the world. A very common saying is, "When in Rome, do as the Romans," but that does not apply to the Christian. No matter where you find him, he is to walk as a heavenly man, as one whose interests are really in another world, as a stranger and a foreigner to this world. He is called to refrain from everything that would in any way tarnish his pilgrim character.

"Walk not as other Gentiles walk, in the vanity of their mind." The word translated "vanity" here does not mean what it does ordinarily—that is, "pride." The original word rather means something like a mirage, an illusion, that which is imagined but not actually true. Unsaved men have illusions of the minds, they see mirages of all kinds and imagine them to be real, but they are not. They believe all sorts of theories, intellectual ideas, and such like, and would even judge God's Word by their theories instead of judging their theories by the test of God's Word. These poor Christless men, whatever their talents, culture, or education, have never been born of God, therefore their understanding is darkened, and they are incapable of understanding divine things. The Christian ought to be aware of this danger, and not walk in the delusions of the fleshly mind.

"The natural man receiveth not the things of the Spirit of God" (1 Corinthians 2:14). I wish our Christian young people would realize that. Many of them who are attending our colleges and universities are placed under the instruction of brilliant but unconverted professors who use their position to undermine faith in the Word of God. I wish these Christian young men and women could realize that the natural man, no matter what his intellectual qualifications, does not understand the things of God; they are foolishness to him because they are spiritually discerned (1 Corinthians 2:14). Without a new life and a new nature there can be no real comprehension of divine things, and so the greatest of this world's scholars is an ignoramus when it comes to the things of God, until he has been regenerated.

Paul described the Gentile world of his day: "Having the understanding darkened, being alienated from the life of God through the ignorance that is in them, because of the blindness of their heart" (Ephesians 4:18). In other words, they have no divine life. Some say there is a divine spark in every man, but that is not true. "He that hath the Son hath life, and he that hath not the Son of God hath not life." Until Christ is received by faith, until people have accepted Him as their own Savior and Lord, there is no life whatever except, of course, this material, natural life. Paul continued his description, "Being alienated from the life of God through the ignorance that is in them." They are wise in the things of this world, but utterly ignorant in the things of God "because of the blindness of their heart." The word *blindness* is better translated "hardness," and yet that does not give the thought sufficiently. It means a heart that is under the influence of an anesthetic. A person may be alive and quivering with pain, but when he is put under the influence of an anesthetic he is not awake to his true condition. Men and women have come under the influence of the awful deadening power of sin and their hearts are hardened. They are blinded, and they do not understand their own condition, the condition of their country, or of the world around them. Sin has a terrible, hardening, blinding, deadening, effect on people.

Notice the awfully graphic picture of the ancient world and the world today. "Who being past feeling have given themselves over unto lasciviousness, to work all uncleanness with greediness" (19). "Being past feeling," might be translated, "being beyond pain." Do you remember how pained you were the first time you committed some sin that pricked your conscience? The hour of temptation came, and you hesitated and said, "Shall I commit this sin or not?" Conscience was roused and you did not see how you could go on and indulge in that evil, unholy thing. But perhaps lured on by godless friends who mocked your conscientious scruples, you said, "Oh, I'll try anything once," and you took the fatal step—you committed that sin and polluted your soul by it. But you remember the pain that came afterward, you remember as you walked home, or possibly it was in your own home, you could not bear the thought of facing those nearest and dearest to you. Perhaps you were not so much concerned about the fact that God had seen you, but you were concerned about what others might think of you. The temptation came a second time and again you plunged into the sin, more recklessly this time, and afterward the pain was less. And so on and on and on, and now you continue in that sin, in that evil course, and there is scarcely ever the least evidence of a sensitive conscience. We read of people whose conscience is seared as with a hot iron. In Ephesians 4:19 we have the description of an unsaved man going contrary to every divine direction until he is beyond pain. That is what sin does for people. Oh, what a mercy when the Spirit of God comes in and awakens one to see something of the terribleness of his sin in the sight of a holy God. Then the Spirit leads the repentant sinner to Christ, and out of the depths of an anguished heart he cries, "What must I do to be saved? God be merciful to me, the sinner." There had been such crises in the lives of these Ephesians. Many of us have known what this means, and now these words of instruction come to us, as to them, regarding the manner of life that should characterize us.

We are not to be as we once were and as those still are who, having lost their sensitivity to pain, have given themselves over to lustful desires and all kinds of unholy thoughts resulting in unclean works. What a mercy that this is in the past for many of us. Am I speaking to anyone who is still living in these things? Does your heart sometimes cry out with a desire for purity, for holiness, for goodness? Do you sometimes say:

> Tell me what to do to be pure
> In the sight of all-seeing eyes.

Tell me, is there no thorough cure,
No escape from the sins I despise?

Will the Savior only pass by,
Only show me how faulty I've been?
Will He not attend to my cry?
May I not this moment be clean?

Oh yes; there is cleansing for you. "Come now, and let us reason together, saith the Lord; though your sins be as scarlet, they shall be as white as snow; though they be red like crimson, they shall be as wool" (Isaiah 1:18). God has made His invitation so clear. The heart of the sinner may be made pure. There is a possibility that the dark red stains of sin may all be washed away, for it is written, "The blood of Jesus Christ [God's] Son cleanseth us from all sin." And one cleansed by the blood should be characterized by an altogether different life from that which is common to the unsaved.

The apostle continued, "But ye have not so learned Christ; If so be that ye have heard him, and have been taught by him, as the truth is in Jesus" (20-21). I want you to notice particularly the way he used the divine titles. We know that Jesus is Christ and Christ is Jesus. We do not for one moment consent to the wretched theory that a good many hold today, popularized by Christian Science, which tries to draw a distinction between Jesus and Christ. According to that system, Jesus was simply a man, the natural born son of Mary, but Christ was a divine Spirit that came and took possession of Jesus at His baptism in the Jordan. That is an old gnostic heresy condemned by every right-minded Christian. Jesus is the Christ. "Whosoever believeth that Jesus is the Christ is born of God." But although that is true, this is also true—Jesus was His human name here on earth; He never had that name until He came to earth. Scripture says, "Thou shalt call his name Jesus; for he shall save his people from their sins" (Matthew 1:21). But He was *Christ* from all eternity. In the eighth chapter of Proverbs, wisdom is personified, and we read, "The Lord possessed me in the beginning of his way, before his works of old. I was set up from everlasting, from the beginning, or ever the earth was" (22-23). The Hebrew term *set up* is the same word for *anointed*: "I was the anointed One from everlasting." When Christ was baptized in the Jordan, the Spirit of God descended on Him confirming that He was the anointed One, the Christ from eternity. And when God raised Him from the dead, we read He made that same Jesus to be both Lord and Christ (Acts 2:36). He is the Anointed now as the risen and glorified One.

Paul was thinking of Christ as the risen One, sitting at the right hand of God, and we learn of Him as we take time to truly look at Him. "But we all, with open face beholding as in a glass the glory of the Lord, are changed into the same image from glory to glory, even as by the Spirit of the Lord" (2 Corinthians 3:18). But what does Paul mean by "the truth is in Jesus"? He means that when He was on earth as the lowly man called *Jesus* He was the demonstration of the truth. That is why He could say, "I am the way, the truth and the life." Suppose I want to know the truth about what God expects from man, where do I find it? In Adam? Oh, no. In Adam I see a man who listened to his wife, after she listened to the devil, and did what she told him to do. Adam was a man without a backbone, a man utterly untrustworthy. As we review human history, we see that all humanity is just a reproduction of that first man. But if I want the truth concerning man and his relationship with God, I find that it is written, "There is...one mediator between God and men, the man Christ Jesus." As we read God's Word and notice Christ's attitude and behavior when He was on earth, we see all that man should be for God. He is the full standard of humanity.

If I want to know the truth about God, where do I find it? Do I go to the universities of this world? No; they do not know anything about God. They cannot tell me anything about Him. But where shall I go? To the modernistic churches, with their unconverted preachers? They do not know anything more about God than unconverted college professors. Well, then, where shall I go? To Creation? Out in the woods? No, you will not learn about God there. you will get some evidences of His power and wisdom, but you will not find anything about His love and holiness there. Where do you learn about Him? In Christ. "He that hath seen me hath seen the Father." The truth has been made known in Jesus.

Suppose I want to find out about sin, where will I go? To some of our modern, humanistic philosophies whose teachers talk about behaviorism and actually try to make men and women believe that every tendency within the heart is perfectly lawful and perfectly right? No, not there. But where? To the cross of Jesus. There, as I behold my blessed Savior taking the sinner's place, I see what sin deserved. The truth is in Jesus, and Christ in glory points me back to Jesus on earth and says, "If you want to know how you should walk as you go through this world, there is where you will find it." "Christ also suffered for us, leaving us an example, that ye should follow his steps" (1 Peter 2:21).

But how will I be able to live like this? I have an old nature; I once had a corrupt, sinful life, how am I going to live like Jesus? Here is what Jesus teaches: "That ye put off concerning the former conversation the old man, which is corrupt according to the deceitful lusts; And be renewed in the spirit of your mind; And that ye put on the new man, which after God is created in righteousness and true holiness" (Ephesians 4:22-24). What do I mean when I speak of the old man? Some people confuse the old man with the old nature. You see, the old man is more than the old nature. The old man is what you once were before you were converted. Now you are through with the old man. If you are a Christian, you are not to live like that man any longer, but you are now to live in the righteousness and holiness of the new man. And who is the new man? The new man is the man of whom the apostle Paul speaks in 2 Corinthians 12: "I knew a man in Christ...of such an one will I glory." A man in Christ—that is the new man that I now am through infinite grace. I am through with the old man, the man after the flesh. I have put him off, his tastes, his appetites, all that he once delighted in, and I am learning the truth as it is in Jesus.

The old man was "corrupt according to the deceitful lusts," and in our unconverted days we lived to satisfy these deceitful lusts. But now a great change has taken place, we have been born again. That does not mean we have attained perfection. The apostle Paul said:

Not as though I had already attained, either were already perfect: but I follow after, if that I may apprehend that for which also I am apprehended of Christ Jesus. Brethren, I count not myself to have apprehended: but this one thing I do, forgetting those things which are behind, and reaching forth unto those things which are before, I press toward the mark for the prize of the high calling of God in Christ Jesus (Philippians 3:12-14).

"And be renewed in the spirit of your mind" (Ephesians 4:23). A better rendering is, *"Being* renewed in the spirit of your mind." In what sense am I being renewed in the spirit of my mind? How am I being renewed in my physical strength? I am strengthened physically by eating those foods that are nourishing and that will build a strong body. Then how am I renewed in the spirit of my mind? I am strengthened spiritually by feeding on His Word, enjoying communion with Him and fellowship with His beloved people. In all these ways we are being renewed in the spirit of our minds. You never saw a strong Christian who was not a Bible-loving Christian. You never saw a strong Christian who was not one who delighted in communion with fellow believers. People who don't want anything to do with other Christians, and go about with an "I am better than you" attitude, do not exhibit much real holiness in their lives.

We read that the new man "is created in righteousness and true holiness." Righteousness is my behavior toward others. I am to be righteous in my dealings with my fellow man. As a new man I cannot be careful about my devotion to Christ while being careless in my life among others. A man got up in a meeting one day and said, "I want to tell you that I am standing in Christ on redemption ground." Another man arose and said, "I want to call that man down. He says he is standing in Christ on redemption ground. I do not believe a word of it. He is standing in a pair of shoes he bought from me months ago, and he has not paid for them yet." Righteousness is right dealing between men. The person who professes to be a Christian and is not careful about that which is right, is a disgrace to the name of the Lord Jesus Christ.

Holiness has to do with my attitude toward God. It is in the heart; it is the inward life, holiness of thought. Holiness is seen as a heart separated to God in accordance with the truth of His holy Word. This is practical Christianity, and this is how you and I are called to exhibit the new life, to reveal the fact that we belong to a new creation.

Have I been setting the standard too high? I have not been setting it at all. I have been showing you the standard as set in the Word of God.

Unsaved one, are you saying, "I would like to reach this standard, but I do not see how I ever could"? You cannot. With all your trying you will never be able to reach it. Come to God as a poor, lost sinner, give up your trying, put your trust in the Lord Jesus Christ, and He will give you a new heart, a new nature, and will enable you to live to His glory.

Grieve Not the Holy Spirit (4:25-32)

The most important part of this entire section is verse 30, "And grieve not the Holy Spirit of God, whereby ye are sealed unto the day of redemption." The word *grieve* means "to give pain." Give not pain to the Holy Spirit of God. How do we pain Him? By walking in disobedience to any of the admonitions that are given us in this particular section. We have here the behavior that should characterize a believer. We have seen something of our wonderful privileges, our great blessings in Christ in the heavenlies, and now we are considering that part of the Epistle that underscores our practical responsibilities.

It is a poor thing to talk of living in the heavenlies if we are walking with the world. It is most inconsistent to glory in our privileges in Christ if we are living according to the flesh. And so in these verses the apostle emphasized the importance of true Christian living. He wrote, "Wherefore putting away lying, speak every man truth with his neighbour; for we are members one of another" (25). We have seen that as we look at the exalted Christ in glory our hearts turn back to consider the example set us by Jesus as He lived in this world and embodied all truth. The Jews came to Him on one occasion and said, "Whom makest thou thyself?" (John 8:53) And He said (using the exact rendering), "Altogether what I say unto you." What a tremendous statement. He covered nothing; He hid nothing. In Him there was no sham, no pretense; He was exactly the same in the presence of God as He was before men. This indeed is truth in life, and you and I who have put our trust in Him are called to put away everything that is false.

The word translated "lying" is simply the Greek word that we have taken over into the English, *pseudo*—"that which is false." We are to put away everything that is merely pretense or sham, and speak the truth with our neighbor. The Christian is called to be punctilious, to be honest even in little things, not to make bargains that he does not keep. A Christian business man should not overstate his case when he is trying to sell something. In Proverbs we read, "It is naught, it is naught, saith the buyer: but when he is gone his way, then he boasteth" (Proverbs 20:14). Deception on the part of the buyer is also contrary to the Holy Spirit of God. The Christian is called on to be true in everything; true in his behavior, true in his speech.

Notice the motive given for speaking the truth, "For we are members one of another." Paul is thinking especially of our relation to fellow believers, as though he would say, "Why do you attempt ever to deceive a fellow believer? Why do you lie to another child of God? Why do you pretend to something that is not true when dealing with another Christian? Why are you unfaithful to a member of the same body to which you yourself belong?" Can you imagine the various parts of our natural bodies being false to one another? What is for the good of one is for the good of all; and so in the body of Christ, what is for the good of one member is for the good of all. The Christian is called to see that he never defaults in any way in his dealings with a fellow Christian.

Then we read in verse 26, "Be ye angry, and sin not: let not the sun go down upon your wrath: Neither give place to the devil." This verse has perplexed many people. Some imagine that it is always wrong to be angry. There are circumstances under which it would be very wrong not to be angry. Our Lord though absolutely perfect in His humanity was angry on more than one occasion. He saw the pretentious Pharisees going in and out of the temple of God with a great air of sanctity. Yet He knew some of them held mortgages on widows' homes, and when occasion arose they foreclosed on them and turned the widows out into the streets because they could not meet their obligations. Our Lord's indignation was aroused, His anger flamed up, and He said, "Woe unto you, scribes and Pharisees, hypocrites! for ye devour widows' houses, and for a pretence make long prayer: therefore ye shall receive the greater damnation" (Matthew 23:14). If my spirit would not be stirred to indignation by this kind of behavior today, I am not the sort of Christian I ought to be. If I am not stirred to anger by seeing the helpless oppressed, I am not a Christian. There is an anger that is righteous. We read that our Lord Jesus on one occasion "looked round about on them with anger, being grieved for the hardness of their hearts." How, then, am I to be angry and sin not? A Puritan has put it this way, "I am determined so to be angry as not to sin, therefore to be angry at nothing but sin."

You see the moment *self* comes in to the situation, my anger is sinful. You do me a wrong and I flare with anger. That is sinful anger. But you blaspheme the name of my Savior and if I am not stirred to anger, that is sin. If I am reconciled to God as I should be, it will arouse my indignation when I hear His name blasphemed, or see His truth dragged in the dust. But so far as I am concerned, I am to suffer all things, I am to endure all things. Men may consider me the refuse of the earth, they may do the worst they can against me, but if I become angry, I sin, for self is the object there.

Who is there then that is sinless? No one; that is why Paul said, "Let not the sun go down upon your wrath." If you are stirred to sinful anger, if you flare up, see then that you do not go to bed at night before you confess your sin. If you have lost your temper before another, see that you confess it to him and ask forgiveness. Many people have said to me, "I have such a bad temper. I have tried so hard to overcome it, but I get angry and say things that I regret afterwards. Then I make up my mind never to do it again, but I always fail." I usually ask this question, "Do you make it a practice, when you have said angry words, to go to the person you have sinned against and confess it?" Sometimes I get this answer, "No, I never hold anything in my heart; I flare up, and then it is all over." The memory may be over for you, but the memory of that anger is not all over. The other person remembers it. If every time you sin through anger you would go immediately to the one sinned against, and confess and ask forgiveness, you would soon get tired of going so often and you would check yourself. It would not be so easy to fly off the handle. But as long as you can flare up and pay no attention to it, or while you may confess it to God you do not do so to your brother, you will find the habit growing on you.

This expression, "Be ye angry, and sin not," is a direct quotation from the Septuagint translation of Psalm 4:4. The King James version reads, "Stand in awe, and sin not: commune with your own heart upon your bed, and be still." The Hebrew word translated "stand in awe" is a word that means "tremble"—tremble at the presence of God. But this is not necessarily all that it means. These words were probably recorded at the time that David was fleeing from Absalom, his own son, and his heart was stirred as he thought of his son's disrespectful behavior. That son for whom he had so often prayed was bringing dishonor on the name of the Lord, and it moved his heart to indignation. But he said, "I am not going to sleep tonight until all that indignation is quieted down—'Stand in awe, and sin not: commune with your own heart upon your bed, and be still.'" In other words, Just get quietly into the presence of God and then you will be able to look at things from a right standpoint. As you think of your own failures, of the many, many times that God in grace has had to forgive you, it will make you very lenient as you think of the failures of others. Instead of rising in judgment on another believer, it will lead you to self-judgment and that will bring blessing. Anger and a refusal to forgive will only harm your own spiritual life.

"Let not the sun go down upon your wrath: Neither give place to the devil." Why? Because anger cherished becomes hatred, and Satan works through a hateful spirit. He seeks to get control of Christians and have them act in malice toward fellow believers. All this grieves the Holy Spirit of God. These are searching truths, and we have to take them each for himself. "the word of God is quick, and powerful, and sharper than any twoedged sword, piercing even to the dividing asunder of soul and spirit, and of the joints and marrow, and is a discerner of the thoughts and intents of the heart" (Hebrews 4:12). Let us not avoid facing our anger honestly.

"Let him that stole steal no more: but rather let him labor, working with his hands the thing which is good, that he may have to give to him that needeth." There is many a person who steals who would not like to be called a thief. We have names for stealing that sound much better, for instance, *pilfering* and *cheating*. They mean the same thing but do not sound quite as bad as *stealing*. But the Spirit of God covers them all in the command, "Let him that stole steal no more." Let him that appropriated that to which he had no right, steal no more. The Christian is to be intrinsically honest.

It is easy to become lazy along these lines. For instance, if you are working in an office you may say to yourself, "Oh well, they don't pay me anything near what I am worth, so I have a right to certain little things around the office." I knew one young man who had a habit of stealing pencils until he had accumulated a gross of them, and then his conscience smote him. One day he had to go back to the boss with the pencils and say, "I am a Christian and I am returning these pencils to you." Christians are called to be faithful in very small things, things that others may not pay any attention to at all. What a pity that sometimes Christians cannot be trusted. The child of God ought to be the one who can be trusted anywhere, one who will be faithful in another man's things just as much as in his own things.

But it is not enough that we refrain from thievery. The law says, "Thou shalt not steal," but grace comes in and sets a much higher standard than that under law! It is not only, "Let him that stole steal no more," but Paul added, "but rather let him labor, working with his hands the thing which is good, that he may have to give to him that needeth." I could live up to the righteousness of the law if I refrained from stealing, but I cannot live up to the holiness of grace until I share with others what God in His kindness gives to me. What a wonderful standard is that of Christianity.

Next Paul exhorted his readers regarding their manner of speech: "Let no corrupt communication proceed out of your mouth" (29). The Psalmist said, "Set a watch, O Lord, before my mouth; keep the door of my lips" (Psalm 141:3). And James said, "If any man offend not in word, the same is a perfect man, and able also to bridle the whole body" (James 3:2). I have met some "perfect" people; I knew they were perfect because they told me so. But when I was with them a while and listened to their speech—heard their careless, worldly chatter, noticed how critical of other people they were, heard the unkind, cutting remarks they could make concerning other people—I knew their perfection was all a delusion. "If we say that we have no sin, we deceive ourselves and the truth is not in us."

What did Paul mean by "corrupt communication"? Corrupt communication comes from the old corrupt nature. The new nature produces holy communication. "Let no corrupt communication proceed out of your mouth, but that which is good to the use of edifying [that is, for the building up of those to whom you speak], that it may minister grace unto the hearers." "Oh," says somebody, "this is where my trouble is. My tongue is always getting me into difficulty. I make up my mind never to say anything unkind, and the next minute my tongue seems to be set on a pivot." Very well, when you find that you just must talk and you cannot stop, say, "Now, Lord, this tongue of mine wants to get going; help me to say something good." And then quote some Scripture and speak of the grace of the Lord Jesus Christ. Speak of that which will build up your hearers, and you won't go away with regrets and at the close of the day have to get down on your knees and say, "O Lord, forgive me for my careless chatter and un-Christianlike words today." We are not made to be silent; some of us like to talk. But we are to talk about good things. We are to let Christ be the center of our speech, to present Him to others.

I have known men with whom it was a delight to spend a little time because I never left them without having learned more of the Lord Jesus. I am thinking of a friend of mine in whose company I have never been for more than ten minutes before he would say to me, "You know, I was thinking of such and such a Scripture, and while I was meditating the Spirit gave me such and such a thought." How different it is with others at times. How different it has been many, many times with my own tongue. What sorrows it has brought on me when I have spoken unadvisedly.

And now we come to the crucial text—"And grieve not [pain not] the holy Spirit of God, whereby ye are sealed unto the day of redemption." As we have already seen, the Spirit of God dwells in each believer. As a divine Person and heavenly guest, He is listening to everything you say and is taking note of everything you do. All that is said and done contrary to the holiness of Christ and to the righteousness of God, grieves that indwelling Holy Spirit. Have you ever known what it was to have someone in your home who did not approve of something you were doing? Perhaps nothing was said but you had the sense that this person was not pleased. That is the way it is with the Spirit of God if a believer is not walking in accordance with the truth.

Do we read, "Grieve not the Holy Spirit of God, lest you should grieve Him away?" No, you are not going to grieve Him away. Jesus said, "I will pray the Father, and he shall give you another Comforter, that he may abide with you for ever" (John 14:16). When He comes to indwell a believer, He never leaves. David, in the Old Testament dispensation, said, "Take not thy holy spirit from me." But in the glorious dispensation of grace, that prayer is unnecessary, for when He comes to indwell us He never leaves us until we are presented faultless in the presence of the Lord Jesus Christ. The point is just this, that although He dwells within us and does not leave, He is grieved all the time that we are walking in disobedience to the Word. That is why many of us are never very happy; that is why we do not enjoy communion with God and sing songs of victory. As long as the Holy Spirit dwells in me ungrieved He is free to reveal the things of Christ to me, and that fills my heart with gladness. But the moment I begin to grieve Him He stops doing the work He delighted to do, He is not free to open these things to me. He has to convict me of my own failure and sin until I confess it.

Then, I have the joy of knowing that I am sealed—how long? "Unto the day of redemption." What does Paul mean by that? Is not the day of redemption the day Christ died on Calvary's cross? That was when Jesus died to redeem my soul. But there is the coming day of the redemption of the body when the Lord will return again to transform these earthly bodies and make them like His own glorious body. It is the redemption referred to in Romans 8:22-23:

> For we know that the whole creation groaneth and travaileth in pain together until now. And not only they, but ourselves also,

which have the firstfruits of the Spirit, even we ourselves groan within ourselves, waiting for the adoption, to wit, the redemption of our body.

We are sealed until the redemption of our bodies. When our bodies are redeemed, the old nature will be gone, we will not have to be on our guard any more against grieving the Holy Spirit. It is here and now in this body that we need to watch against this.

Paul concluded this section of Ephesians 4 by saying, "Let all bitterness, and wrath, and anger, and clamour, and evil speaking, be put away from you, with all malice." I wish that as Christians we would be obedient to this word of God! Is there any bitterness in your heart against anyone on earth? Do you say, "but you don't know how I have been tested, how I have been tried, insulted, offended?" If you had not been offended there would be no reason for the bitterness at all, but Paul said, "Let all bitterness, and wrath, and anger, and clamour, and evil speaking, be put away from you, with all malice." If you do not live up to that, you are not living a real Christian life. This is Christianity lived in the power of the Holy Ghost.

We are not merely told to put these sinful things away, but there is also the positive side of the command: "Be ye kind one to another, tenderhearted, forgiving one another, even as God for Christ's sake hath forgiven you." To what extent must I forgive? "I have forgiven over and over and over again, and I cannot go on forgiving forever," you say. Wait a minute. What does the apostle say about the extent to which we are to forgive? "Even as God for Christ's sake hath forgiven you." Can you ever forgive others more than God has forgiven you? Has anyone ever wronged you as much as you have wronged God? But if you have trusted the Savior, God in Christ has forgiven you all your trespasses. Now this is the standard for Christians, we are to forgive one another even as God in Christ has forgiven us.

EPHESIANS 5

Clean Christians (5:1-7)

The city of Ephesus swarmed with iniquity of the vilest kind. It was therefore of great importance that the early Christians should be warned of the danger of following the ways of those still in their sins. And it is just as necessary today. The human heart is unchanged and with all our veneer of civilization, unmentionable depravity is seen throughout our land. The wickedness of the world is enough to cause every Christian heart to shudder and realize the importance of living very close to the Lord Jesus Christ that we may be kept from these evil things.

Notice that the basis of the apostle's call to clean living is found in the closing words of Ephesians 4: "as God for Christ's sake hath forgiven you." God thought enough of us to send His only begotten Son into the world to reconcile us to Himself. He took our place and bore our shame. He endured the judgment due to our sins—because of this, let us walk now in such a way as to express the gratitude of our hearts for this great salvation. "Be ye therefore followers of God, as dear children."

The word rendered, "followers," really means "imitators." "Be ye therefore imitators of God." In what sense are we to imitate God? One thinks of a passage in the Old Testament where God commanded His people, "that they put out of the camp [of Israel] every leper"— that is, everyone who had any kind of an infectious disease. This was done not only for the safety of those who were not yet infected, but also to preserve the holiness commanded by the law: "Ye shall be holy: for I the Lord your God am holy." And as in the legal dispensation all physical uncleanness was considered a curse, making the unclean person unfit for the holy presence of God, so today all sin of the flesh and spirit must be eliminated if we would walk in fellowship with the holy One. We are called to imitate Him in holiness of life, imitate Him in purity of thought, and imitate Him in cleanness of speech as His dear children in whom He takes pleasure.

You parents know how there are times when your own children, much as you love them, cause you sorrow and grief if they walk in disobedience and bring dishonor to the family name. So it is with God's children. The least sin indulged in by His children grieves the Holy Spirit. If we would be His dear children, in the sense of children in whom He can delight, we must be imitators of God and "walk in love, as Christ also hath loved us, and hath given himself for us an offering and a sacrifice to God for a sweetsmelling savour." The reference in this verse is to the burnt offering described in Leviticus 1. The offerer came to God with a sacrifice, not merely to atone for sin he had committed, but because his heart was filled with thanksgiving and he wanted to present an expression of his loving adoration. And so there is one aspect of the work of our Lord Jesus Christ on the cross that rises far above the mere meeting of our need; it has in view the glorifying of God in this world where He has been so terribly dishonored.

The Lord Jesus said to His disciples on the last night in which He was betrayed as they sat with Him at the table, "That the world may know that I love the Father; and as the Father gave me commandment, even so I do. Arise, let us go hence" (John 14:31). And He went out to die. Why did He endure that death on the cross? His first object was the glory of the Father. God had been terribly dishonored by the first man and all that had come after him, but here at last was a man who walked in this world in absolute holiness. He said, "I seek not mine own will, but the will of the Father which hath sent me" (John 5:30), and to do the will of God He went to that cross. He went there to settle the sin question for us, but above everything else it was to show that at least one Man had been found to whom the glory of God meant more than anything else. The will of God meant more to Christ than any personal desires that He Himself might have had. And so in Gethsemane's garden we hear Him saying, "Nevertheless not as I will, but as thou wilt." This is the great burnt offering. He offered Himself without spot *to God* a sacrifice of "sweetsmelling savour." But we are not left out. He offered Himself *for us*. And since we have thus been redeemed, we ought to live holy and godly lives.

"But fornication, and all uncleanness [impurity], or covetousness, let it not be once named among you, as becometh saints" (Ephesians 5:3). The sensitive soul is shocked by these terms describing the vilest corruption of which the human heart is capable. They are given that we may realize that all these sins must be judged if we would now walk with Him who has redeemed us to God. The word rendered "covetousness" does not refer here to greed for money, but sensual greed. It is a disgusting greed for sensual gratification, the vilest thing of which the human heart is capable. Is it possible that saints of God need to be warned against these things? Yes, because in every believer there is the same corrupt nature that there is in the man or woman of the world. It is true that the saint has received a divine nature and the Holy Spirit of God has come to dwell in him, but nevertheless, he must always watch against the least stirring of that old nature lest he fall into sin.

Sexual immorality is in the very air around us. Modern literature is full of it, and the worst of it is that people glory in their vileness. But some say, "Well, our modern writers are very frank; they show up sin as it really is." Yes, they are disgustingly frank in the way they speak of it, and yet they seem to throw a halo around it as though these unclean things are so natural to human beings and no one need be ashamed of them. And the world is fast getting to the place our Lord Jesus Christ predicted it would be just before His second coming. He said, "As it was in the days of Noah, so shall it be also in the days of the Son of man" (Luke 17:26). The days of Noah were days of great corruption and violence, and we are living in very similar times. All of our boasted civilization has not changed the tendency of the human heart one iota, and the child of God is to guard against every evil tendency. The first approach to sin is always in the mind, and so God warns against indulging in impure thoughts. We are to guard against lust of every description. Can you think of any greed more dreadful or disgusting than that which would lead one to plot the ruin of an innocent young person's life? It breaks the hearts of parents who have tried to raise their precious children in the right way, when someone entices them away from the path of goodness and purity. Can you think of anything more dreadful than an attempt to break up a happy home by coming between husband and wife, turning one or the other aside from the path of faithfulness? And yet these things abound everywhere. This is the greed about which the apostle warns us. The pathetic fact is that people look with such indifference at these things.

After warning against immorality, the apostle continued, "Let it not be once named among you, as becometh saints." It is even defiling to talk about it, even to pass on the news that other people have fallen into those sins. If as servants of God we have to deal with such things, we find it necessary to get into the presence of God in prayer, for they leave their effect on our hearts and minds.

Notice what we read in verse 4, "Neither filthiness, nor foolish talking, nor jesting, which are not convenient: but rather giving of thanks." Every word in this verse needs careful consideration. The apostle is not warning us against bright, happy conversation that leads people sometimes to exchange agreeable thoughts and lively clean humor. He is not calling us to be long-faced, unhappy people who do not dare to tell anything that provokes an innocent laugh. In fact, I am rather afraid of people who are so holy that they cannot laugh. A good, hearty laugh is a healthy thing. God meant man to laugh. That is the one thing that distinguishes us from all the other creatures. God rejoices over His people. The apostle is thinking here about that kind of humor which is more subtle and dangerous. Every Christian needs to be on guard againt it.

"Neither filthiness," that is, indecency—do not talk of indecent things. "Nor foolish talking," which really means crass joking, talking like a fool about unclean things. You know people who think it witty and smart to tell vulgar jokes and use words with double meanings, words that cause an innocent person to blush or enter the mind as a stumblingblock. *Foolish talking* literally means, "a fool's talk," and the man who talks this way demonstrates that he is a fool. The word *jesting* is really *ribaldry*, and is another word that implies in a deeper sense joking about things that should never be even talked about. Christians should be clean like their blessed Lord—clean in thought, in word, and in deed.

In place of these things, what should occupy the Christian tongue? "Rather giving of thanks." There is a beautiful play on words in the Greek language that does not come out in the English. The word translated "jest" and the term "giving of thanks" begin exactly the same. The Greek for the one is *eutrapalia*, the Greek for the other is *eucharistia*. The apostle was balancing the one word against the other. Not *eutrapalia* but *eucharistia*; that is, not ribaldry but thanksgiving, not vile talk but praising the Lord, not filthy conversation but that which brings glory to the Lord Jesus Christ.

On one occasion I was attending a conference of Christians and a number of us were guests at the home of a very devoted believer. As we gathered between meetings one day in the beautiful living room, a lady suddenly said, "Let's go out and see if our hostess would like some help getting the dinner ready." After the women left the room, about fifteen men remained together. A man who had just come in remarked, "Since the ladies have left, there is a story I heard today that I would like to tell you." Before any one else had a chance to speak, a friend of mine said, "Just a minute, brother; there are no ladies here, but the Holy Spirit is here and He is more sensitive than the most fastidious lady. Is your story fit for Him?" The man was big enough to say, "Thank you, Mr. B—, I accept the reproof. I will never tell such a story again." Remember, the Holy Spirit of God is grieved if believers stoop to any of the things mentioned in this verse.

Next, the apostle warned that if any reject this instruction and live in uncleanness, they simply give evidence that they are not Christians at all. They are children of the devil, merely wearing the uniform of the Christian. "This ye know, that no whoremonger, nor unclean person, nor covetous man, who is an idolater, hath any inheritance in the kingdom of Christ and of God" (5). Why does he couple idolaters with these other people? Because this kind of person worships only himself. What does he care if he breaks other people's hearts? What does he care if he wrecks young lives or breaks up homes? He must satisfy his own base cravings. He worships one god; that god is himself. It is absurd for a man like that to profess to be a Christian.

Those of us who are ministers of Christ have heard the stories of hundreds of broken-hearted young women who have come to us. They have told us of their betrayal, of the breaking down little by little of their higher ideals and the ruin that has come. I feel the greatest punishment that their betrayers could bear would be to have to listen forever to these sad stories and know that they were responsible for them. I have had fathers and mothers come and sit weeping as they have talked of a child who was once the joy of their home, the love of their hearts, and tell how that child had been lured away into sin. Their hearts were broken and they could no longer find the joy in their child they once did. I have said, "If these betrayers of the innocent would only have to sit and listen to stories of this kind year after year, it would be a fitting punishment." And some of these betrayers profess to be Christians! Sometimes they are in the church. More shame to them, coming under the cover of the church and pretending to be what they are not while continuing in their depraved, sinful way! Christians ought to be clean and pure because they are children of the holy One, the holy God.

"Be not ye therefore partakers with them" (7). While we may pray for them, there is to be no fellowship with them, no condoning of their sinful deeds. They should be made to feel that they are unclean lepers until their sins are confessed and judged, and they have given evidence of being delivered from them. As Christians we are to walk in love, that love which would never cause us to harm anyone else, but always to seek the good of others with Christ as our example. "As Christ also hath loved us, and hath given himself for us an offering and a sacrifice to God for a sweetsmelling savour."

You may say, "But what if some have fallen into such sins; is there no hope?" No hope until the sin is judged; no hope until it is confessed. There is no hope until with sincere desire to be completely delivered from it they turn to Him who is the Holy and the True, and cast themselves in repentance and faith on His atoning work. Then, trusting Christ, they will find that He gives them a new heart and a new life, and makes them lovers of purity and goodness.

The Fruit of the Light (5:8-14)

This section immediately follows the exhortation to personal purity. The clear light of God's holiness is to be our standard. "Ye were sometimes darkness, but now are ye light in the Lord: walk as children of light" (8). Notice that he does not say, "Ye were sometimes in the dark," but, "Ye were darkness." Darkness is ignorance of God, and we were once, in our unconverted days, in ignorance of God and therefore said to be "darkness." We did not have the Light of life. Every natural man is in that condition. Zophar asked Job the question, "Canst thou by searching find out God?" (Job 11:7) And the answer is in the negative, for all philosophizing or reasoning about divine things ends in confusion because men in their natural state are darkness.

"The natural man receiveth not the things of the Spirit of God; for they are foolishness unto him" (1 Corinthians 2:14). They are spiritually discerned. We were once in that condition, and when in that darkened state, we walked in darkness, and practiced things of which we are now ashamed. But having become children of the light, being born of God and made light in the Lord, we are to walk as children of the light.

In the first chapter of John we read of our Lord: "In him was life; and the life was the light of men." Did you ever stop to meditate on those words? Divine life was fully revealed in our Lord Jesus Christ, for He was "that eternal life, which was with the Father, and was manifested unto us" (1 John 1:2). John said, "The life was the light of men," or, as he puts it in another place, "That was the true Light which coming into the world casts light on every man" (John 1:9, literal translation). Even if He uttered not a word, His pure and holy life, always in obedience to the Father, was in itself the condemnation of all sinful men. "The life was the light." You and I are children of the light, and we possess that same life which our Lord Jesus Christ is. He is the eternal life and He has communicated eternal life to us. That life is now to be shown as light.

A lady said to me some time ago, mentioning a certain servant of Christ, "Did you ever know Mr. so and so?" "Oh, yes," I said, "I knew him well." "Well," she said, "you know, we had him in our home for a month and his very presence there seemed to change everything for us. Why, there was such godliness about him. He was reverent but not sullen. He showed holiness without gloominess. Our children simply loved him, and yet there was such intense godliness that soon the little things that they used to do and say carelessly, dropped away. They did not like to say in his presence what they would when he was not there; when he was looking they did not like to do those things that ordinarily they would do with utter indifference. The effect of his presence in our home was simply wonderful and yet he never reproved anybody by word of mouth for anything they did or said, but he displayed the life, and the life was the light." We have known the other kind of people also.

I have had the privilege of having in our home all sorts of Christians. Some of them were loved by our children and were always welcomed because of their Christlikeness and devotedness. Others have caused the children to gnash their teeth when they saw them coming up the walk. I can recall one good man who seemed to think it was his business to run our house when he was there. If a child was a little slow to obey or a bit flippant, as children sometimes are, instead of leaving the discipline to his parents, he would exclaim, "That child ought to be spanked!" You can imagine the effect on the children. You can imagine how they loved to hear a man like that preach, how they would want to see him as a visitor in our home! It is not the person who goes around constantly finding fault with other people who accomplishes the best results. He only stirs up the flesh and arouses the hatred of the natural heart to things that are pure and good. But the man who lives Christ, the woman who exhibits life eternal in the home, among friends, in the church, these are the people whose testimonies really count for God. "The life is the light."

You remember how the apostle Peter emphasized the purity of life when he addressed wives who have unconverted husbands. He said to them in 1 Peter 3:1-4:

> Likewise, ye wives, be in subjection to your own husbands; that, if any obey not the word, they also may without the word be won by the conversation of the wives; While they behold

your chaste conversation coupled with fear. Whose adorning
let it not be that outward adorning of plaiting the hair, and of
wearing of gold, or of putting on of apparel; But let it be the
hidden man of the heart, in that which is not corruptible, even
the ornament of a meek and quiet spirit, which is in the sight of
God of great price.

I wonder if women these days have ever noticed this passage.
Peter was speaking of a woman who had been brought to Christ,
and her husband was still in paganism or Judaism, as the case may
be, and she was deeply concerned over his conversion. What was to
be her attitude? Constantly nagging and talking and reproving? Oh
no. Her behavior is to be so sweet and Christlike and gracious that
as he looks at her he will say, "Well, my wife has something now
she did not have before. She used to be so ready to speak up and
talk back, and now she is so sweet and gracious. I wonder what it is
that she now possesses that is so contrary to what characterized her
by nature."

"If any obey not the word, they may also without the word be
won." In the first clause *the word* is the Word of God that is meant.
In the second instance it means verbal nagging. The verse might be
paraphrased thus: "Likewise, ye wives, be in subjection to your own
husbands, that if any obey not the Word of God they also may without nagging be won by the good behavior of the wives." And the
same principle applies to every one of us. It is not merely something for women to consider. We men are also called on to live the
truth we profess, not by constantly finding fault with people, not by
criticizing and trying to set everybody and everything right by the
words of our mouths, but by manifesting the life of Christ, the purity of Christ, the love of Christ in our lives. This is what Paul meant
when he wrote, "walk as children of light."

"For the fruit of the light" (in the King James version it is, "The
fruit of the Spirit," but several other translations read "light") "is in
all goodness and righteousness and truth" (Ephesians 5:9). Here
then are the graces that should characterize those who are children
of light. It is not enough to profess to believe on the Lord Jesus
Christ, to submit to Christian baptism, to take communion at the

Lord's table, to be members of some Christian assembly or congregation, but we are required to show the fruit of the light in our lives. Where there is life there is fruit. Where there is only a dead profession you will not find fruit, but where people are truly born of God there will be fruit. "By their fruits ye shall know them." "Even a child is known by his doings, whether his work be pure, and whether it be right" (Proverbs 20:11). Children who have made a profession for Christ are responsible to produce the fruit of the light, and if they act in a willful or wayward manner they should immediately go to the Lord and confess it. Their lives should be different from the lives of other children who have not yet accepted Christ. Whether young or old we are to manifest the fruit of the light.

What is this fruit of the light? "For the fruit of the [light] is in all *goodness.*" The word literally means "benevolence, kindly consideration for other people." If you are really born of God, you possess a new and divine nature, you will follow the footsteps of the Lord Jesus Christ, and of Him we read, "The Son of man came not to be ministered unto, but to minister, and to give his life a ransom for many" (Matthew 20:28). "He laid down his life for us: and we ought to lay down our lives for the brethren" (1 John 3:16). "We *ought.*" That is a word that speaks of duty. "To lay down our lives for the brethren"—that is the opposite of selfishness. The world says, "Number one first," but we are called by God to be considerate of others first. Someone has well said that heavenly grammar is different from worldly grammar. In ordinary linguistic form the three persons are, first person, *I*; second person, *you*; third person, *he* or *she*. But in Christianity it is: first person, *he* or *she*; second person, *you*; and third person, *I*. In Christianity I come in last; I am not to put myself first. When I am thinking of comforts, I am to think of others first. But how different it is with many of us. We are content if we do a little from time to time to alleviate the suffering of others, whereas we are called to live for Christ daily and to manifest the *goodness* of the light continually.

And then in the second place, "The fruit of the [light] is in all...righteousness." *Righteousness* is simply doing right. What an amazing exemplification of the unrighteousness of the human heart we have seen within the last few years! Trusted officials in banks, big businessmen who were respected and thought to be absolutely reliable, have in many instances proven to be unrighteous men handling other people's money dishonestly, unfaithful to their trust. What a lot of suicides have followed our bank failures. How fast our penitentiaries are filling up with men who a short while ago were considered dependable. Yet our modern theologians are still dreaming that human nature is not corrupt, and that "every fall is a fall upward."

A friend of mine riding on the streetcar handed the conductor a gospel tract. When the conductor's busy time was over, he walked down the aisle of the car to my friend and said, "You handed me this?"

"Yes."

"Why did you give it to me? I have no interest in these things."

"But that is a gospel message."

"I don't need the gospel. It is for sinners, but I don't believe in sin, and I don't believe that man is a fallen creature."

"That is peculiar," my friend said. "Why have you that machine at the door of the car?"

"Oh, that is to count the money."

"But why do they need it for men like you in whom there is no sin?"

Theologians can talk about an improved race and a sinless race and deny the fall of man, but businessmen know differently. The rule today is, "Do not trust anyone until he proves that he is not a cheat." Christian, be careful about attempting to witness for Christ by word of mouth if you are not displaying the fruit of the light in your life. Be sure that behind your testimony there is a righteous life.

Finally, "The fruit of the [light] is in all...truth." Righteousness has to do with your actions towards others. Truth has to do with your own inward sincerity. "Thou desirest truth in the inward parts: and in the hidden part thou shalt make me to know wisdom" (Psalm 51:6). Years ago when I was a young Salvation Army officer, on one occasion our colonel came to address us. Quite a group had come in from all over the state for an officers' council. I have never forgotten through all these years the faithful words of the colonel.

He said, "Now remember, friends, people will forgive you if you are not educated; they will forgive you if your culture is not up to the highest standards, if you are not eloquent, if you cannot sing beautifully. But they will never forgive you if they find out that you are not sincere, that you are pretending to be what you are not." When Christ dwells in us, we will be real, we will be genuine in our dealings with God and with men.

"Proving what is acceptable unto the Lord." In other words, "Testing what is acceptable unto the Lord." We should not be so ready to compromise and say, "I think this is all right; I do not see any harm in that," and run off to do as we will. Our first thought should be, "I am a Christian and the Holy Spirit of God is living in me. Is this what Christ would have me do? Will this bring glory to my Lord? If I say this, if I do that, if I go here, will I really be honoring my Savior?" In that way we "test what is acceptable unto the Lord."

Then we are admonished to "have no fellowship with the unfruitful works of darkness, but rather reprove them" (11). As we have already seen, we prove our faith by the lives we live. The Christian cannot expect to be kept from contamination by sin and evil if he continues in fellowship with iniquity. You might as well expect a child to play in the filth and grime of the streets and not get dirty, as to expect a Christian to go on in fellowship with sin and not be affected by it.

This verse together with many others have exercised my own conscience through the years and kept me from a great many associations into which I would otherwise naturally have gone. When years ago I considered joining certain secret societies and lodges, the question at once arose, Are they composed of born-again people? If I do join them, will I be having "fellowship with the unfruitful works of darkness"? Will I be walking in the path laid down for me by Christ? For the Lord has said, "Come out from among them, and be ye separate,...and touch not the unclean thing; and I will receive you, And will be a Father unto you, and ye shall be my sons and daughters" (2 Corinthians 6:17-18). That Scripture kept me out of many questionable circles. But I have gained immensely, for the time I would have spent in some of those associations I have been permitted to spend with the people of God or over the Word of God.

Do not be afraid that you will ever lose by obedience to God's holy Word. The strength of the Christian is in his separation from the world and his devotion to Christ.

Paul said that we are to reprove the works of darkness. By this he did not mean mere cricital fault-finding, as is evident from the words of verse 13: "All things that are reproved are made manifest by the light." That is what is needed. Just turn on the light and it will show up everything that is contrary to it. In other words, you live the pure, holy, Christlike life, and that in itself will be reproof enough of the sin that is so prevalent in our world today. "All things that are reproved are made manifest by the light: for whatsoever doth make manifest is light." John wrote in his first Epistle, "God is light, and in him is no darkness at all." Light is the very nature of God, and the moment one comes into the presence of God he is exposed as a sinner. But there in the presence of God he sees the precious blood on the mercyseat reassuring him that his sin has been atoned for and put away. Thus he enjoys peace with God as he walks in the light unafraid because he is in Christ.

The danger is that all this may become merely head knowledge. "Wherefore he saith, Awake thou that sleepest, and arise from the dead, and Christ shall give thee light" (14). It is not possible to find any one Old Testament Scripture that contains these words in their exactness. They are rather a free translation of Isaiah 60:1. There the Spirit of the Lord speaking through the prophet says, "Arise, shine; for thy light is come, and the glory of the Lord is risen upon thee." The apostle takes that word *arise* to mean, "wake up out of your sleep." He is calling Christians to wake up, just as when you go into your child's room in the morning and say, "It is time to wake up!" Many who profess to be Christians are like people sleeping in a cemetery, sleeping among the dead with their heads pillowed on the gravestones! You who are children of the light (this is not a message for the unsaved but for those who are saved and have gone to sleep): "Awake...and arise from the dead, and Christ shall give thee light." "Come out from among them, and be ye separate." Show by your life that you are different from the unsaved worldly people around you.

Do you want blessing? Do you want a sense of the light of His face shining on your life? Do not tolerate any hidden wrong; confess it and turn from it. Maybe it is a letter you ought to write, maybe an acknowledgment you ought to make, maybe some money you ought to return. Do you say, "I can't afford it"? But it is not yours. Put things right and then trust God for the rest. Righteousness first, and other things will follow. "Awake, thou that sleepest, and arise from the dead, and Christ shall shine upon thee."

The Filling with the Holy Spirit (5:15-21)

In these verses we continue considering the walk of the believer: "See then that ye walk circumspectly, not as fools, but as wise." This is the seventh verse in which the word *walk* occurs in this Epistle (KJV). I think it will be profitable to go back and notice the occurrences of this word.

In chapter 2:2 we have the past tense: "Wherein in time past ye *walked* according to the course of this world." In that verse the apostle was speaking of how we used to live when we belonged to the world. But we who are saved are delivered from that and so we read in verse 10 of the same chapter, "For we are His workmanship, created in Christ Jesus unto good works, which God hath before ordained that we should *walk* in them." We are not saved by good works, but we are to do good works after we are saved. In chapter 4:1 we read, "I therefore, the prisoner of the Lord, beseech you that ye *walk* worthy of the vocation wherewith ye are called." Having been called with a heavenly calling, we are now to walk—behave ourselves—as a heavenly people. Following that, in verse 17 of the same chapter we read, "This I say therefore, and testify in the Lord, that ye henceforth *walk* not as other Gentiles walk, in the vanity of their mind." In our unconverted days we walked in the pride and folly of the human mind in conflict with God, but as believers we are not to do this any more. We are to live humble lives, obedient to the Word of God. Then in chapter 5:2 we are told to, "*Walk* in love, as Christ also hath loved us, and hath given himself for us an offering and a sacrifice to God for a sweetsmelling savour." In verse 8 we read, "Ye were sometimes darkness, but now are ye light in the Lord: *walk* as children of light." And now we are considering verse

15 where the apostle said, "See then that ye *walk* circumspectly, not as fools, but as wise."

Our English word *circumspectly* means "looking all around," like one who is walking in a very dangerous place. There are pitfalls on this side of the path, quagmires on that side, traps and snares all around. And so the person walking on this path is constantly observing where he should next place his feet. That is a *circumspect* walk—a walk looking all around. Christian, your path leads you through a world of sin and foolishness, a world where you are exposed to all kinds of temptations and unholy influences. Snares and traps are everywhere set for your unwary feet. Therefore, walk circumspectly, be careful where you put down your feet; be careful as to the company you keep. Be careful as to your behavior in any company, so that you will bring glory to the Lord Jesus Christ. Walk not as fools, not as simple ones, not as those who are still darkness, but walk as wise men—made wise by the wisdom of God.

"Redeeming the time, because the days are evil." The apostle used this expression in one of his other letters (Colossians 4:5). In each instance it literally means, "Buying up the opportunities." Just as people go out bargain hunting and finding something on sale say, "That's a good price for this article. I should buy this article today while it is at this price. That would be much better than waiting until later." Let the Christian be just as eager and sincere to obtain opportunities to witness for Christ, to serve the Lord, and to be a means of blessing to others with whom he comes in contact. We are to be buying up opportunities to bring glory to our Lord Jesus, realizing that the days are evil and the time for serving Christ is slipping fast away. Opportunities once lost will never be found again, therefore the importance of buying them up while we are able.

"Wherefore be ye not unwise, but understanding what the will of the Lord is." It is important to remember that the only way you and I can be delivered from our own natural foolishness, is by being divinely enlightened. We do not understand what the will of the Lord is until we give ourselves to the careful, thoughtful study of His Word. Years ago I often stopped in the middle of a discourse and asked everyone in my audience who had read the Bible through once to raise his hand. The last time I did that I was so ashamed that

I made up my mind never to do it again. I had an audience of five hundred people, all of whom professed to be Christians, and when I put that question to them, only two raised their hands, and I was ashamed to have the devil see it. It seems that Christians do not value their Bible very much any more.

I am reminded of something that occurred in Chicago. There was an open religious forum downtown. Clarence Darrow was there to represent the atheists, another person represented Protestantism, another Roman Catholicism, and another, Judaism. The Catholic got up and told why he was a Catholic; the Protestant got up and told why he was a Protestant; the Jew why he was a Jew. Then Clarence Darrow, the atheist, got up to speak, and he said, "Gentlemen, I have been very much interested in one thing. I notice Protestant, Catholic, nor Jew ever referred to the Bible. Evidently they no longer value that so-called holy Book as they used to do." And then he went on to declare that he was an atheist because he had no use for the book that they never even mentioned. What a pitiable thing that professed Christians should attempt to tell why they were Catholic or Protestant and never once refer to the Bible! Oh, that you and I might be genuine Bible Christians!

A friend of mine used to be called a "walking Bible," and I thought, *What a splendid description*! If anybody ever came to him and said, "Mr. so-and-so, what do you think about such and such a thing?" he would say, "Let us see what God says about it," and out would come his Bible. "Why," the man would say, "I didn't know the Bible had an answer for that question." I never knew this friend to say, "I think," but always, "God's Word says so and so." If you and I would be wise with the wisdom that comes from above, we need to search the Scriptures. I like that little chorus:

> In my heart, in my heart,
> Send a great revival;
> Teach me how to watch and pray
> And to read my Bible.

The pitiful thing is that a great number of Christians are so busy with other things that they have very little time to read their Bibles.

Although engaged exclusively in Christian service now for 45 years, I do not dare come into the pulpit or begin my day's work without first going to the Word of God to gather fresh manna. If sometimes I am so hurried in the morning because of being out very late, or an urgent call comes and I rush out thoughtlessly without going to the Book, I find myself thinking, *What is the matter with me today? I feel so dried up and half-starved spiritually. I am in no condition to try to minister to other people.* Then the answer comes, "Why, you didn't have your spiritual breakfast this morning. You went off without a morsel from God's Word," and I have to say, "Lord, forgive me for thinking that anything is more important than time spent with You."

If you are not in the habit of reading your Bible methodically, prayerfully, let me plead with you, go into the presence of God and confess to Him the sin of neglecting His Holy Word. He says, "Search the Scriptures," and if you disobey a command, it is sin. If you have been disobedient, go to Him and confess it and say, "Lord, teach me to say with Your servant, 'Neither have I gone back from the commandment of his lips; I have esteemed the words of his mouth more than my necessary food'" (Job 23:12). Give God the first place in your life, give His Word the place it should have and then you will understand what the will of the Lord is.

The apostle continued, "And be not drunk with wine, wherein is excess; but be filled with the Spirit" (Ephesians 5:18). You will notice he puts two things in opposition to each other—drunkenness with wine and the filling of the Holy Spirit. Why does he contrast these two conditions? People who have been drinking excessively and become drunk with wine are controlled by a spirit foreign to themselves. When they are under the influence of alcohol, they do and say things that they never would in their normal condition. They make fools of themselves, descending to all kinds of vulgarity and nonsense. Others excuse them, saying, "Oh well, you mustn't hold it against them; they're drunk; they are not themselves." The apostle says that that condition should never be true of a Christian, but on the other hand the Christian should be dominated and controlled by the Holy Spirit of God. In the power of the Holy Spirit one is enabled to say and do what he could not say and do in his merely natural condition. And so the filling of the Holy Spirit ought to be the normal experience of every believer—"Be not drunk with wine, wherein is excess; but be filled with the Spirit." The last clause is more accurately translated, "Be habitually filled with the Holy Spirit."

What is the filling with the Holy Spirit? A great many people think it is some strange, ecstatic, emotional experience that comes to them at a given moment and then later passes away and has to be repeated again. But that is not it. The filling of the Holy Spirit is the normal experience of the Christian life. We read of the disciples that "they were all filled with the Holy Ghost, and they spake the word of God with boldness" (Acts 4:31). They were controlled by the Holy Spirit of God, and this does not necessarily result in any special emotional breakdown, but rather preserves one in the path of orderliness and common sense. In 2 Timothy 1:7 we read, "God hath not given us the spirit of fear; but of power, and of love, and of a sound mind." I have been in some places where people talk a great deal about the fullness of the Spirit and I have seen behavior that I never would have thought possible a few years ago outside of an insane asylum—people rolling around the floor and raving like maniacs—and yet calling that experience the fullness of the Spirit. That is not the spirit of a sound mind. The man who is filled with the Holy Spirit does not go off into some wild, fanatical state, but walks thoughtfully and carefully with God, and his testimony has power with men.

In Colossians 3:16 we read, "Let the word of Christ dwell in you richly in all wisdom; teaching and admonishing one another in psalms and hymns and spiritual songs, singing with grace in your hearts to the Lord." Notice the effect of the Word of Christ dwelling richly in the soul. As we compare this verse with Ephesians 5:18-19 we see that the results in Colossians when the Word of Christ dwells in you richly are the same as that in Ephesians when you are filled with the Spirit. What then is the inference? There is an old rule in mathematics that "things equal to the same thing are equal to one another." If to be filled with the Word is equal in result to being filled with the Spirit, then it should be clear that the Word-filled Christian is the Spirit-filled Christian. As we walk in obedience to the Word of Christ, the Spirit of God fills, dominates, and controls us to the glory of the Lord Jesus Christ. Therefore, if you would be filled with the Spirit and you know of anything in your private life that is contrary to the Word of God, deal with it all before Him. If there is anything in your outward associations, in your behavior before the world that is contrary to His Word, go into His presence, confess your sins—sins of omission and sins of commission. When everything has been uncovered and faced in His presence, dare to believe His promise, "If we confess our sins, he is faithful and just to forgive us our sins, and to cleanse us from all unrighteousness" (1 John 1:9). Ask for His grace to walk in obedience to His truth. Cry out from the depths of your heart as the Psalmist did, "Order my steps in thy word" (Psalm 119:133), and as you walk on in obedience to the Word of God, you will be filled with the Spirit.

You do not need some remarkable outward demonstration or amazing sign that the Spirit of God has actually taken possession of you. Remember that He dwells in every believer, and as you give Him room, He cleanses out of you everything that would hinder His presence. As you let Him take full possession you are filled with the Spirit. What will be the evidence of it? One evidence will be fullness of joy. The Holy Spirit is a Spirit of gladness, the Spirit of joy. Now do not misunderstand me, there is a difference between holy joy and mere natural merriment. For an example we look at the life of our Lord Jesus Christ. Even though He was the Man of sorrows and acquainted with grief, as we read the record of His life in the four Gospels we cannot help but be impressed with the fact that we are not reading the life of a sad man but of a glad man. "In that hour Jesus rejoiced in spirit, and said, I thank thee, O Father" (Luke 10:21). That joy was characteristic of our Lord. In spite of all the grief and sorrow that He bore He was joyful. But having said that, let me remind you that in these records you do not see depicted what the world calls a jolly man. His was no mere worldly merriment, but a deep-rooted gladness that was based on unbroken communion with the Father, and that is the joy that you and I should possess. The one who is filled with the Spirit will be a glad, joyous believer.

"Speaking to yourselves in psalms and hymns and spiritual songs, singing and making melody in your heart to the Lord." As we meet with one another, greeting each other in a glad, happy way, the praises of the Lord bubble up in our souls. Psalms were the vehicle of expression in the congregation of God in Bible times. The book of Psalms was the hymnbook of the congregation of the Lord, and there are wonderful expressions there that suit every mood of the human heart. While we do not rise to the height of the Christian's privilege in the book of Psalms, yet we can find something to express every state and condition of our souls as we come into the presence of God. A hymn is an ascription of praise addressed directly to the Deity. "Holy, Holy, Holy! Lord God Almighty! / Early in the morning our songs shall rise to Thee" (Reginald Heber).

The Christian heart naturally goes out to God in hymns of worship and adoration. No more worldly songs for the Christian. The day is gone, or should be, when he can sing the worldly songs. I always think a Christian has dropped from the high level on which he belongs when I hear him singing such songs, because he has something better—spiritual songs that tell of the love of Christ and His redeeming grace. Who would sing the old songs when we have learned the new?

> We'll sing of the Shepherd that died,
> That died for the sake of the flock,
> His love to the utmost was tried,
> But firmly endured as a rock.
>
> Of Him and His love will we sing,
> His praises our tongues shall employ,
> Till heavenly anthems we bring,
> In yonder bright regions of joy.
>   Thomas Kelly

One reason that the spirituality of the church is at such a low ebb today is because people are so careless about the music that occupies their minds. They are so ready to drop from the high and holy state that should characterize those that are filled with the Spirit of God.

"Singing and making melody in your heart to the Lord." We cannot all make melody on an instrument, but every believer's heart is like a harp. As the Spirit of God breathes over the heartstrings, real melody goes up to the ear of God.

"Giving thanks always for all things unto God and the Father in the name of our Lord Jesus Christ." The Spirit-filled believer will be a thankful believer."Oh but," you say, "there are some things I cannot give thanks for. There are some things so hard and difficult to bear, things that cut my very soul." Wait a moment. Have you ever undergone a serious physical operation as a result of which you have been delivered from some condition that was wearing out your very life? When you had to undergo it, it seemed hard, but as you look back on it, do you not give thanks for the surgeon's knife? Do you not give thanks for the very sufferings you had to endure because of the blessed after-result? Someday, "When we stand with Christ in glory, / Looking o'er life's finished story," we will see more clearly why all the hard things were permitted. We will understand how God our Father was seeking to free us from obstacles and burdens by pruning the branches so that they would produce fruit for Himself. In that day we will thank Him for all the sorrow as well as for all the joy. In faith let us do it now.

Nothing can come to me but what His love allows. "All things work together for good," and so a Spirit-filled believer will be loyal and submissive, not the kind who tosses his head and says, "I am not going to have anybody dominate me; I will do what I think and what I like." That is the old life of our unconverted days; that is the old nature, not the new.

"Submitting yourselves one to another in the fear of *Christ*," as a better translation reads. Christ was God manifested in the flesh. The Spirit-filled believer is characterized by these three things: joyfulness, thankfulness, humility. May God fill each one of us with His Spirit.

The Christian Family (5:22-33)

It is a remarkable thing that in the letter to the Ephesians Paul begins with the highest heights of divine revelation, then in the closing portion he seems to descend to what we might consider very commonplace. He opens his letter with that which thrills our souls—our predestination according to the riches of God's grace to a place that angels have never known. He writes of our lofty position as accepted in the Beloved, blessed with all spiritual blessings in heavenly places in Christ. Then he applies this wonderful body of truth to the behavior of a Christian family. It is a poor testimony to talk high truth while living on a low level in the home. I am afraid there are those who can repeat very glibly the statements of the first half of the Epistle to the Ephesians and delight in the wonderful privileges of the people of God, but fail wretchedly when it comes to living the practical truth of the last half of this Epistle in their daily lives.

You will notice how closely verse 22 is linked with verse 21: "Submitting yourselves one to another in the fear of God." This is a principle of Christian living that applies to believers in every relationship of life, and now that the apostle turns to consider the Christian family he shows that it applies there. Did you ever stop to think what a wonderful institution the Christian family is? In reading a letter from a missionary in a heathen land I was struck by a paragraph that read something like this:

How we wish that some Christian people could come and live among us, even if not to engage in missionary work. There are different ways by which one might make his living among this semi-civilized people. For instance, we might have a Christian dentist and his wife, or a Christian worker in leather—a shoemaker or harnessmaker—with his wife and family. It would mean a great deal to us to have a harmonious family join us here, for we can conceive of nothing that could so commend Christianity to our people as just to see a Christian family living according to the New Testament: a Christian husband loving and honoring his wife, a Christian wife living in sweet and beautiful subjection and loyalty in her home, Christian children who really delight in obedience to their parents, parents who love their children and seek to bring them up in the nurture and admonition of the Lord. This would be so utterly different from anything our people have ever known.

In many heathen lands one cannot find families that function according to Biblical principles. It is the knowledge of Christ that produces the Christian home, and how jealously we should guard this blessed and delightful institution.

After admonishing his readers to submit "one to another in the fear of God," the apostle immediately applies that principle to the relationship of the husband to the wife: "Wives, submit yourselves unto your own husbands, as unto the Lord." The words, "submit yourselves" in verse 22 are not found in the best manuscripts. Let us read verses 21-22 as they are in the Greek: "Submitting yourselves one to another in the fear of God, wives unto your own husbands." He is not calling on the wife to take the place of a slave—she often takes that place in pagan lands—but he is calling for mutual loyalty, mutual respect, mutual submission. Pass over the intervening words to verse 25, "Husbands, love your wives, even as Christ also loved the church, and gave himself for it." That is how the husbands submit themselves to the wives, so it is a mutual thing. That which makes the Christian home what it ought to be is this mutual loyalty, the one to the other—the wife to the husband, the husband to the wife. This is a marvelous principle when you think of it.

For example, we see a young woman who has had her own way to a large extent; she has made her own way through the world. Or she may have come from a home where she has been carefully nurtured and cared for. One day she meets a man and her heart is moved to love him. She says, "I could go to the ends of the world for him. I could keep house for him, care for our children, and submit to him." Or we see an independent bachelor who has made his own way in the world. He has supported himself and could do what he would with his money and time. But one day he meets a woman and is moved to love her. He says, "I could work to support her even if it means I would have to change my life for her. I want to share my life with her." That is the Christian ideal. When the Spirit of God dwells in each heart, the relationship becomes a beautiful picture of the mutual relation of Christ and the church

The same experience takes place in the spiritual world. We see a person living his life utterly independent of God. Then one day he is brought face to face with Christ, and his heart says, "For His sake I resign my own way; I give Him control of my life; I trust myself to Him. I am willing for His name's sake to go and do whatever He would have me do." Christ on His part laid down His life to purchase the one He loves, and now delights to lavish blessings on this one whom He has made His own. We will never fully understand this relationship until we get to Heaven. He has designed that every Christian home should exemplify this very thing.

Do our homes harmonize with this beautiful picture that the apostle brings before us here? Let us examine each verse somewhat carefully. "Submitting yourselves one to another in the fear of God, Wives...unto your own husbands, as unto the Lord." Remember, that the apostle was giving these directions to Christian families. This is marriage not only in the flesh but in the Lord. What a sad thing for the Christian ever to contemplate marriage apart from submission to the Lord. "Be ye not unequally yoked together with unbelievers," is an admonition that applies here as well as to many other relationships of life.

"For the husband is the head of the wife, even as Christ is the head of the church: and he is the saviour of the body." Our Lord as the head of the church provides and cares for all of its needs. So the Christian husband is not to lord his position over his wife in a harsh and arbitrary way, but to exemplify the gracious care of the Lord Jesus Christ as the savior of the body. And so the Christian husband takes on the responsibility to support his wife and his family. He is ready to work hard that they may be kept in a measure of comfort and ease. Because of this, as the church is submissive to Christ so should the wife be to her own husband.

On the part of the husband we read in verse 25: "Husbands, love your wives, even as Christ also loved the church and gave himself for it." A young fellow who had recently become married came to me in distress one day and said, "Brother Ironside, I want your help. I am in an awful state. I am drifting into idolatry."

"What is the trouble?" I asked.

"Well, I am afraid that I am putting my wife on too high a pedestal. I am afraid I love her too much, and I am displeasing the Lord."

"Are you indeed?" I asked. "Do you love her more than Christ loved the church?"

"I don't think I do."

"Well, that is the limit, for we read, 'Husbands, love your wives, even as Christ also loved the church, and gave himself for it.' You cannot love more than that. That is a self-denying love, a love that makes one willing even to lay down his life for another."

We are reminded of the striking story about the wife of one of Cyrus's generals who was charged with treachery against the king. She was called before him and after trial condemned to die. Her husband, who did not realize what had taken place, was apprised of it and came hurrying in. When he heard the sentence condemning his wife to death, he threw himself prostrate before the king and said, "O Sire, take my life instead of hers. Let me die in her place!" Cyrus was so touched that he said, "Love like this must not be spoiled by death," and he gave them back to each other and let the wife go free. As they walked happily away the husband said, "Did you notice how kindly the king looked upon us when he gave you a free pardon?" "I had no eyes for the king," she said; "I saw only the man who was willing to die for me." That sacrificial love is the picture that we have in Ephesians. That should characterize the Christian husband—willing to give even his life for the blessing of his dear ones.

The apostle can scarcely speak about marriage without being reminded of the One who has won his own heart, and he must tell us more about Him. This blessed Husband, this glorious Head of the church, this ideal for every Christian husband, gave up His own precious life for the bride of His heart, the church, "that he might sanctify and cleanse it with the washing of water by the word." Some imagine that this is a reference to baptism, a kind of sacramental washing. But I understand these words to mean that when He has found us in our sins and uncleanness, unfit for association with Him, He applied the water of the Word of His truth to us and we were sanctified by the truth. We were made fit to enter into communion with Him, the holy One. If my hand becomes dirty, I wash it in water and the dirt disappears. So when my conscience, my heart, my life were all defiled, the Lord by the Holy Spirit applied the truth of His Word to me. I was regenerated by the washing of water, and thus made clean in His sight, and so fitted for union and communion with Him.

The full regeneration will be seen in glory when He will present His bride to Himself, a glorious church not having spot caused by sin, or wrinkle caused by age. In Revelation 21:2 we read, "And I John saw the holy city, new Jerusalem, coming down from God out of heaven, prepared as a bride adorned for her husband." This is the glorious picture of the church as it will be throughout all the ages to come—"not having spot or wrinkle, or any such thing." There are some of my brethren who in their hyper-dispensational teaching read this chapter and deny that the church is the bride of the Lamb. They tell us that Israel is the bride. But in Ephesians Paul said the Bridegroom is our Lord; the church, His redeemed spouse, and the two are linked together for eternity. He then applied this principle to our lives again, "So ought men to love their wives as their own bodies. He that loveth his wife loveth himself." The two have become one, and therefore the man who would treat his wife unkindly is as one who would destroy or injure his own flesh. We may also reverse the analogy. We have heard of wives who are so vixenish in their tempers that they cause even good and devoted husbands terrible anguish. Both are one flesh, and need to learn that, "No man ever yet hated his own flesh; but nourisheth and cherisheth it, even as the Lord the church." For so intimate is our union with Him that "we are members of his body, of his flesh, and of his bones."

If some insist that the church is the body but not the bride, the argument that the apostle used contradicts them. The church is both the body and the bride even as a man's wife is both his body and his bride. And so the apostle quoted from the book of Genesis: "For this cause [because of this union] shall a man leave his father and mother, and shall be joined unto his wife, and they two shall be one flesh." What a marvelous union it is when two are brought together through divine grace, the Lord having first united their hearts to Himself and then to each other, and so they set up a Christian home.

Is your home such as the apostle is here depicting, where husband and wife walk together in mutual love and submission, and where Christ is honored? If not, it would be well to ask why it is not. Perhaps you would find that the true root of the trouble is in the neglect of family devotions. In 1 Peter 3:7 we read, "Likewise, ye husbands, dwell with [your wives] according to knowledge, giving honour unto the wife, as unto the weaker vessel, and as being heirs together of the grace of life; that your prayers be not hindered." Notice the words, "that your prayers be not hindered." When a Christian home is the way it should be, prayer like fragrant incense will rise unhindered to God the Father from that family altar. But where the home is not as it should be, where husband and wife are not submissive to God and one another, where there is not that delightful relationship, then prayer immediately is hindered. The family altar is the thermometer that shows what conditions are in the home. What a blessing when husband and wife can happily kneel together and bring their varied problems to the Lord, or together lift their hearts to Him when things are going well. But when there is reserve on the part of either one or the other, you may know there is a storm in the offing, or something has already taken place hindering their fellowship and communion.

If in your home time is not given for the family altar, see to it that not another day goes by until husband and wife read the Word together and kneel together in the presence of God, commending one another and the children to the Lord. You will find it will make a great difference, and day by day anything that would hinder prayer can be judged at the family altar.

In closing this section of Ephesians 5, the apostle said, "This is a great mystery." He has spoken again and again of mysteries in this Epistle. In chapter 1:9 he said, "Having made known unto us the mystery of his will." In chapter 3:3-5 he said, "By revelation he made known unto me the mystery…Which in other ages was not made known unto the sons of men, as it is now revealed unto his holy apostles and prophets by the Spirit." And in this chapter he wrote, "This is a great mystery." Here he was speaking of the mutual relationship of husband and wife. This relationship exemplifies the very mystery that he has been speaking of in the previous chapters: "This is a great mystery: but I speak concerning Christ and the church." There you have the mystery made clear: Christ as the husband, the church as the wife; Christ as the head, the church as the body. This is the marvelous mystery that was not made known in other ages, but has now been fully revealed in the pages of the New Testament.

Of course we understand that the word *mystery* as used here never means something hard to comprehend. It is not mystery in the sense of being something mysterious and difficult to understand. It is rather a sacred secret that the human mind never would have figured out without divine revelation. In the Old Testament times nobody thought of this wonderful truth, the mystery of Christ and the church, but it was revealed first to the apostle Paul and then to others of the New Testament company. It is the great truth that you and I are called on to confess and acknowledge in this dispensation of the grace of God.

We are not to be so carried away by the symbolic truth behind the marriage relation that we forget the obvious truth of the relationship between husband and wife. So the apostle drops again from the mystery itself to the commonplace things of life and says, "Nevertheless let every one of you in particular so love his wife even as himself; and the wife see that she reverence her husband." There is to be mutual love, respect, and loyalty. The wife, while respecting her husband, is to serve in her particular capacity to make the Christian home what it ought to be. The husband, while loving his wife, is to take the responsibility of providing for the family as the acknowledged head of that home. Both are to act in the fear of God. It is Christian homes all over the city, all over the nation, that will strengthen the gospel that is preached from the pulpit. People must see the truths of Scripture lived out in life, and realize the power of Christ to bind two hearts together in such a way that they can exhibit the mutual relationship of Christ and the church.

EPHESIANS 6

The Christian Household (6:1-9)

In these nine verses we have the conclusion of that section of the Epistle which begins with verse 22 of the previous chapter. We have considered the instruction given to Christian wives and husbands in chapter 5 and now we come to consider other members of the family, or the same persons in other relationships.

The apostle spoke first to children. Of course, he spoke directly to Christian children for they alone may be expected to obey the Word of God. This is one way in which children may glorify God and bring honor to the name of the Lord Jesus Christ in their early formative years. As they mature they launch out into the world to make a place for themselves and take part in public service for Christ. "Children, obey your parents in the Lord: for this is right." The apostle considered the matter of obedience correct and proper— "this is right." You profess to be a Christian, young man or woman, well then, here is the first admonition your Lord and Savior gives you, "Obey your parents." Why? Because it is the right thing to do. In the Epistle to the Colossians, where you have the same admonition, it is based on another ground. "Children, obey your parents in all things: for this is well pleasing unto the Lord" (Colossians 3:20). Do you say sometimes, as some Christian children do, "I would like to do some big thing for Christ. I would like to have my life really count for Him"? Well, obedience, the recognition of parental authority and loving submission is well-pleasing to Him. In Luke 2:51 we read that Jesus "went down with them, [that is, Mary and

165

Joseph] and came to Nazareth, and was subject unto them." Here you see our blessed Lord Jesus, the eternal Son of God, become the example for all Christian children. What a wonderful thing! If you are a boy or girl in the home and have trusted the Lord Jesus, you can say, "My Lord was once a child like me. He once had the same position in His home that I do and He filled it well. He was obedient and submissive to His parents in all things." The wonder of it is that He, the Creator of the universe, took that place of subjection, giving us an example that we should follow His steps. Later on as you grow up and go into life you will have Him as your example in other areas of your life, but now He is your example in the home. Christian children ought to take this to heart.

It is a most inconsistent thing for a child to profess to be a Christian, to have his name on the roll of some church, to be in fellowship with an assembly of saints, even taking part in the Lord's supper, and yet be characterized by willfulness and disobedience in the home. There is nothing more distressing, and in some senses more disgusting, than to see a child who claims to be a Christian outside the home but behaves and acts as anything but one in his home. Disobedience to parents is one thing about which God's Word speaks most sternly. In Romans 1, where the apostle is describing the sins that prevail in the heathen world, you will find disobedience linked with the worst kinds of sin. In verses 29-30, we read:

> Filled with all unrighteousness, fornication, wickedness, covetousness, maliciousness; full of envy, murder, debate, deceit, malignity; whisperers, Backbiters, haters of God, despiteful, proud, boasters, inventors of evil things, disobedient to parents.

Notice that disobedience to parents is linked with the vilest immoralities, even with the crime of homicide. The reason for this is that if children are not taught to obey when they are young, they will not obey God, and will not obey the powers that are ordained of God when they go out into the world. That judge in Gary, Indiana was right who, when executing sentence on some young culprits, said, "I wish it were possible to put the parents of these children in the penitentiary for allowing them to grow up like this." As Christian parents we are responsible to see that our children are obedient. And as Christian children we are responsible to obey our parents.

When we turn to Second Timothy 3 we read the apostle's description of the apostasy in the last days. Again he spoke of disobedience to parents as one of the obvious evils of the times: "This know also, that in the last days perilous times shall come. For men shall be lovers of their own selves, covetous, boasters, proud, blasphemers, disobedient to parents, unthankful, unholy" (2 Timothy 3:1). In Romans 1 we have the sins that characterized the heathen world when Christianity began; in 2 Timothy 3 we have the sins that will characterize Christendom at the very end immediately before the coming of our Lord Jesus Christ, and in each case disobedience to parents is listed.

In Ephesians 6:3 the apostle reminded us that the fifth commandment of the law, which commands obedience to parents, is marked out in a special way. In the law we read, "Honour thy father and thy mother; that thy days may be long upon the land which the Lord thy God giveth thee" (Exodus 20:12). As you read the ten commandments you notice that four of them have no special promise attached, and then you come to the fifth and you find that God added a special promise. It shows the importance that He attaches to obedience to parents.

How important, then, that Christian children should take this to heart. Do not be content with lip service; do not be content with attending Sunday school and church and youth group meetings, and think that these things constitute Christianity. First learn to show godliness at home. It is in the home circle that your life is under closest inspection, and it is there you are called on to give evidence of your second birth by obedience to your parents.

Then in verse 4 the apostle speaks to fathers. He did not address himself here particularly to mothers. He said, "Ye fathers, provoke not your children to wrath." Fathers are more inclined to become impatient and unduly harsh and unkind with their children. Yet let me quickly point out Hebrews 11:23: "By faith Moses, when he was born, was hid three months of his parents." The word *parents* there is exactly the same Greek word that is translated "fathers" in

Ephesians 6:4. Fathers and mothers are in this sense addressed together, and so the admonition is given to all parents with perhaps particular emphasis being placed on the fathers. As Christian parents, have in mind your children's well-being, and do not be needlessly demanding of them. Do not lay on them burdens that are too hard for them to bear. Remember that just as children have the Lord Jesus as their example, you have God Himself as yours.

We read, "Like as a father pitieth his children, so the Lord pitieth them that fear him" (Psalm 103:13). Let your attitude toward your children be in accordance with His attitude toward you, and of Him it is written, "He doth not afflict willingly nor grieve the children of men" (Lamentations 3:33). How we need to take this admonition seriously. Paul continued, "but bring them up in the nurture and admonition of the Lord." Parents are to set an example of what a Christian should really be, ministering the Word of God to their children, praying with them, and walking before them consistently, in the fear of the Lord.

I remember the bitterness with which a young woman came to me and said, "I am in the greatest spiritual distress, and the saddest thing about it is that I cannot consult my own father who is a minister of the gospel. But I never remember him praying with his family, and I never knew him to read the Word of God to us. He kept all of his religion for the pulpit, and we never saw any of his godliness in our home." It is in the home we are called first to exhibit godliness, to give prayer and the Word of God their proper place. Let the grace of Christ be seen in your life, and though everything else should go, your children will have the memory of godly parenting and pious upbringing. What an anchor that has been to many a young person launching out in life.

In verse 5, the apostle turned to consider another relationship. He spoke to servants, whether they be in the home or employees outside of the home. The word *doulos*, translated here "servants," means "slaves"—those who are purchased. But you notice in verse 8 he is thinking not merely of the purchased slaves, "Knowing that whatsoever good thing any man doeth, the same shall he receive of the Lord, whether he be bond or free." And therefore the instruction which in times past was given to slaves now applies to all employees. Slaves were bought by a master, or born into the house and raised by the master. But today we enter into an employer-employee agreement. We sell our labor, and in that way accept a certain relationship which makes us just as responsible to obey the command given in Ephesians. There would never be trouble between management and labor if the Word of God were valued more highly in all our hearts and lives. However, it is not expected that unsaved men will heed this admonition, but Paul was addressing Christian employees. "Servants, be obedient to them that are your masters according to the flesh, with fear and trembling, in singleness of your heart, as unto Christ." The fear we are to have is the fear of not giving proper service to our employer, and so of grieving the Holy Spirit of God.

This gives great dignity to labor! Whether a man is working in a factory, or an office, whether he is a miner in the bowels of the earth, or a farmer working on the surface of the earth, each may say to himself, "I serve the Lord Christ." When Carey applied for foreign missionary service, somebody said to him, "What is your business?" They intended it as a slur, for he was not a minister. He said, "My business is serving the Lord, and I make shoes to pay expenses." And so every one engaged in any occupation should be able to say, "My business is serving the Lord, and my occupation pays my expenses."

"Not with eyeservice, as men-pleasers." I looked up the word *eyeservice* and found it to be very interesting. It comes from exactly the same word as that translated "servants" in verse 5, and that is, properly speaking, "a slave." Eye-service then would be eye-slavery. Did you ever know anyone who was an eye-slave? The man who pretends to be working until somebody says, "The boss is coming!" The young woman who wastes her employer's time until somebody says, "Look out, the manager is coming through the office." Then she immediately gets busy and the typewriter rattles as it has not done for hours. That is eye-slavery. Do not let there be anything like that with the Christians. No matter what my employment is, I am to do it as unto God from my heart. My job is the place in which He has put me and I am there to labor for Him. This lifts me far above all concern about the failure of an employer to properly recognize my worth. When I know I am working for the Lord and He knows everything, it saves me from all such worries. "Ye are bought with a price; be not ye the servants of men" (1 Corinthians 7:23).

I may have an employer who does not seem to appreciate me at all, who only wants to get all he can out of me and pay as little as possible. But I have sold my labor to him, and therefore I go on and labor earnestly. I say to myself, *Never mind, there is One who does appreciate, and He knows that I am doing this work well and doing it for His glory. Some day I will receive my reward from Him.* "Oh, yes, yes," you say, "that is all very well. Religion is the opiate of the people." People of Communistic tendencies say, "Christians tell the poor to resign themselves to their situation. They tell them that no matter how hard their life is here, it will be all right when they get to Heaven, in order to keep them contented here." Not at all, that is not what the apostle is saying. "Be not deceived; God is not mocked: for whatsoever a man soweth, that shall he also reap" (Galatians 6:7). It is true in this life as well as in the world to come that the one who honestly serves the Lord Jesus Christ is rewarded for it. Many a man can bear testimony to that! One has labored apparently unappreciated for years until suddenly under the hand of God circumstances change so that he is recognized and honored and respected for all his efforts. The Lord often sees to this even in this life; and there is a great deal more coming in the life ahead.

Next Paul turned to the masters, Christian masters, again we have to say. "And, ye masters, do the same things unto them, forbearing threatening: knowing that your Master also is in heaven; neither is there respect of persons with him" (Ephesians 6:9). You masters expect your employees to honor you and recognize their responsibility to rightly serve you. Very well then masters, it is your responsibility to properly consider the welfare of your employees. You have been trusted with wealth or have been put in a position where you administer the wealth of others—see that you do not look upon your employees as mere "hands." Do not treat them cruelly, driving them in order to get the most out of them, and giving them the least. Remember that as they are responsible to serve the Lord Christ, so are you, and you are to do it to His glory.

"Forbearing threatening." Nothing of an unkind, cruel, or discourteous character is to be seen in the Christian master. Remember "that your Master also is in heaven," and therefore you have to give an account for all your dealings with your employees. If you cut down their wages when it is not necessary, if you seek to force them to work under unhealthful and unsanitary conditions, God is looking on and jotting everything down in His book of records. He sees that you behave in an unchristian way toward those dependent largely on you. Christianity equalizes everything. Here is the true socialism, not a leveling of all distinctions, but men and women of every class submissive to Christ. That puts everything right. Your wealth will not accomplish anything if you do not handle it correctly; your authority will amount to nothing if you do not use it for His glory. "Neither is there respect of persons with him." God judges each one according to his own works.

What helpful instructions we have here! How important that every Christian, whatever his relationship, should act according to this truth. In the beginning of this Epistle we have the highest kind of spiritual revelation. There it is that we learn that we have been raised up together and seated together in heavenly places in Christ. "Very well," said the apostle, "if you are a heavenly man, a heavenly woman, a member of the body of Christ, now behave on earth as Christ would if He occupied your position in life, whatever your business may be. Let the Spirit of Christ be manifested in you." This will commend Christianity to a lost world.

We have had too much talking of high truth coupled with low living. We have had too much delight in glorious eternal truths and yet that truth never affecting the feet. "Order my steps in thy word," prayed the psalmist. May God grant that whether as husband or wife, child or parent, employee or employer, we may each one who names the name of Christ show His grace in every relationship of life. May our homes be places where husband and wife together are seeking to glorify the Lord Jesus Christ, each giving honor to the other and seeking to fulfill his or her place in the family, and where the children are growing up in the nurture and admonition of the Lord. May masters and servants alike recognize their responsibility to the great Master in Heaven who was once a Servant here on earth.

In reading the first 9 verses of Ephesians 6 we find ourselves in an atmosphere of peace and blessing not known by the unconverted. When Paul wrote this letter, there were very few Christian homes in the world. But thank God, as a result of the proclamation of the truth during nineteen centuries, all over this and other lands may be found homes that follow the pattern set down here in Ephesians.

If today you are unsaved and you have sometimes stumbled over the inconsistency of Christians, let me say that the Word of God takes it for granted that Christians need constant admonition. But you are invited to come just as you are to Christ, trust Him as your Savior, receive the divine life by faith, and then live as a Christian should, and show the rest of us what a real Christian ought to be. Do not be foolish enough to stumble over anyone else's inconsistency and refuse God's offer of salvation. Remember, there is power to make you what you ought to be—a Christian not in word only but in deed and in truth.

The Christian's Conflict (6:10-12)

As we turn from the beautiful description of the Christian household we immediately find ourselves in an altogether different atmosphere. The apostle has barely concluded his admonition to husband and wife, parents and children, masters and servants, before he speaks of warfare and conflict, for we cannot always enjoy the sweetness and quietness of a Christian home. We have to go out into the world. We have to go out into a life where cruel enemies seek to disrupt and destroy our Christian experience and endeavor in every possible way to lead us to do or say things that will bring dishonor to the name of our Lord. We go from the home to the battlefield.

Earlier in our study we noted the correlation between the letter to the Ephesians and the Old Testament book of Joshua (see Introduction). In the book of Joshua we have the Israelites, a redeemed people, entering their possession, the land of Canaan. In the Epistle to the Ephesians we have believers, moved by the Spirit of God, entering in to possess their heavenly inheritance in Christ. This inheritance is not merely something which is to be ours when we die and leave this world or when our Lord returns, but we are told that here and now we have been blessed "with all spiritual blessings in heavenly places in Christ." There is a grand and wonderful sphere of blessing, which God would have us enter in spirit while we are yet in this physical world.

Many people are accustomed to think of Canaan as representing Heaven after death, and therefore they think of the river Jordan as always representing death itself. If you will stop and think for a moment, you will realize that there is a sense in which Canaan could scarcely represent Heaven, because it was after the people of Israel entered that land that their real conflict began. They found it was already occupied by hostile nations who immediately rushed against them and sought to keep them from the enjoyment of that land which God had given them. When you and I who are saved are finally called away from this world, we are not going to the other side for conflict—we will not find ourselves engaged in battle with evil spirits in Heaven. But as believers in the Lord Jesus Christ, when we seek here on earth to appropriate the blessings that are already ours in Him, we find at once that there is a host of evil powers seeking to prevent us from enjoying the victory that is ours by right of our relationship to the Lord Jesus Christ. Therefore, we can see how Canaan represents primarily our present place of blessing in the heavenlies. The armies of Canaan, disputing Israel's possession, represent what we have in Ephesians 6:12—the principalities and powers, the world rulers of this darkness, who are doing their utmost to keep Christians living on a low, worldly level.

As the apostle closed his letter to the Ephesians we are reminded that we are not yet in Heaven. We have not reached the rest that remains for the people of God, and therefore he wrote, "Finally, my brethren, be strong in the Lord, and in the power of his might." Perhaps it might be translated, "My brethren, be daily strengthened," for it is in the continuous tense; that is, "be constantly receiving strength from the Lord and go forth in the power of His might." It is important to realize that even after we have been converted for many years we have no more power in ourselves to ensure victory over the foe than we had when first saved. The power is not in us but in God, and therefore we need to live in constant communion with Him. The preacher and the choir cannot do their work effectively unless in communion with God. The Christian laborer, secretary, salesman, or farmer cannot defeat the enemy unless they are in communion with God. We all need His mighty quickening power to enable us to triumph in our respective spheres just as much as any missionary going to a foreign field to carry the gospel to lost men and women. Here is a challenge each of us must face, for we cannot overcome in our own strength. Therefore we are reminded of the importance of living near to the Lord, being strengthened in the Lord and in the power of His might.

"Put on the whole armour of God, that ye may be able to stand against the wiles of the devil" (11). This is the armor that we have delineated for us piece by piece in the next section of the Epistle. The armor is from God; it is nothing of ourselves, for we have nothing in ourselves whereby we can meet the foe. Not only in Ephesians but in other Scriptures as well, the apostle by the Spirit insists that we dress appropriately for battle. In Romans 13:11-14 we read:

> And that, knowing the time, that now it is high time to awake out of sleep: for now is our salvation nearer than when we believed. The night is far spent, the day is at hand: let us therefore cast off the works of darkness, and let us put on the armour of light. Let us walk honestly, as in the day; not in rioting and drunkenness, not in chambering and wantonness, not in strife and envying. But put ye on the Lord Jesus Christ, and make not provision for the flesh, to fulfill the lusts thereof.

How many a Christian has forgotten these words and found himself absolutely powerless in the hour of temptation, unarmed, exposed to every imagination of a cruel enemy. "Put on the whole armour of God."

Then again, in 2 Corinthians 10, the apostle wrote of this same warfare. We read that it is not a conflict with the flesh. We are not told to fight the flesh but to reckon ourselves dead to sin in the flesh. Our conflict is with the fallen spirits that dominate this present age of evil. These spirits, of course, cannot indwell believers, but they can do a great deal in the way of alluring believers into paths where they tarnish the name of the Lord. In verses 3-5 we read:

For though we walk in the flesh, we do not war [against] the flesh: (For the weapons of our warfare are not carnal, but mighty through God to the pulling down of strongholds;) Casting down imaginations [or human reason, for Satan works through the mind, getting men to question rather than to believe what God has revealed in His holy Word], and every high thing that exalteth itself against the knowledge of God, and bringing into captivity every thought to the obedience of Christ.

Here, then, is our conflict. We are exposed to these evil spirits who are haters of God and our Savior. Therefore they seek to disgrace that holy name whereby we are called, by leading us off into things that grieve the Holy Spirit and discredit our testimony. How necessary then is the admonition, "Put on the whole armour of God, that ye may be able to stand against the wiles of the devil."

It would be a very simple thing if the adversary of our souls came to us honestly and said, "Good morning. I am the devil, and I want you to get into something that is going to cause you a lot of misery and wretchedness, and which will dishonor your Savior. If you will only listen to me and obey me, I will be able to accomplish this." We would have no difficulty in saying to him, "Get thee behind me, Satan: for thou savourest not the things that be of God, but the things that be of men" (Mark 8:33). But he does not come that way. He is transformed into an angel of light, and he seeks to deceive us. Paul wrote of the *wiles* of the devil. The word *wile* is the same one from which we get our English word *method*, but it implies a subtle method or craftiness. Satan is an old campaigner; he has been at the business of deceiving men and women for at least six millenniums, and he knows exactly how to approach every individual soul as he comes with his crafty method. In every conceivable manner he will seek to hinder us from making progress in our Christian lives and experience, and therefore we need to be constantly on the watch. We are given an illustration of that in Joshua 9.

God had told Joshua to cross over Jordan and that he would find there the seven nations of Canaan. They were corrupt and abominable, given to all kinds of vileness and idolatry, and the Israelites were commanded not to enter into any leagues or marriages with them, but to completely destroy them. The words were plain, and for a time Joshua and the people carried them out implicitly. But one day a strange-looking group of men, dressed in rags, limped up the highway. Their sandals were worn out, and they carried old sacks that contained moldy bread. Their goatskin water bottles were cracked and dried up. Some of Joshua's scouts went out to see them and asked, "Who are you, and what do you want?"

"We would like to see your general," they said.

And so they were led into the presence of Joshua, who inquired, "Well, what is it you want with us? Where do you come from?"

"From a very far country," they said. "You see these clothes of ours. They were brand-new the day we left home and you can realize that we have come a long way. These sandals were bought from the shoe dealer the day we left. This bread was brought fresh from the oven, but now it is all moldy. We have come a long distance because we have heard of you and of how God is with you. We would like to make an alliance with you. Let us be friends. We would be very proud to be linked up with you, and we hope that you will be willing to make an alliance with us."

"This is most interesting," said Joshua; "you say you are from a long way off. How did you hear about us?"

"Oh, the word is going all through the land. We heard of the victory as you entered the land, how Jericho and Ai fell before you. Let us get together and make an alliance."

And we read that the Israelites made an alliance with them and asked not counsel of the Lord. Thus they were deceived by the wiles of the Gibeonites. A day or two after they had made the league, when there was no chance to break it, they found out that these men came from a nearby village and were anxious to join them in order to save their own lives.

How the devil has deceived God's people through the years! One of his first attempts to corrupt the church of God is by getting unconverted people into its fellowship. Today church membership is often largely made up of unsaved men and women. When it comes to public service for the Lord, a great corruption in the church today is that of unconverted people joining together in a choir to professedly sing the praises of the Lord. Choir members who are flirting with the world are just as truly a hindrance to the work of God as the preacher flirting with the world. It is one of the wiles of the devil to try to mix the saved and the unsaved together. Of course there is no blessing when such a condition exists. Oh, that churches today were totally committed to God!

We are to recognize that we are not wrestling against flesh and blood. We have no quarrel with our fellowman, but we are wrestling "against principalities, against powers, against the rulers of the darkness of this world, against spiritual wickedness in high places" (Ephesians 6:12). It might be translated, "Against the world rulers of this darkness." These are the principalities of fallen angels who are marshaled under the skull and crossbones banner of Satan himself. They are the great evil powers—evil angels who are seeking to control the hearts of world leaders, to hinder men and women from submitting to the truth of God. For example, look at the leadership during World War I. Who were the rulers of the world at that time? There was President Wilson, King George of England, Kaiser Wilhelm of Germany, King Victor Emmanuel of Italy. However, they were not the actual rulers of the world; they were simply like the pawns on the chessboard. The world rulers were the wicked spirits endeavoring to influence the hearts of men in an attempt to destroy the human race. So malignant is the spirit of these evil beings spoken of here in the Word of God that we are not competent to meet them until we put on the whole armor of God. We cannot face this enemy and win the battle unless we draw our strength day by day from our Lord Himself, and use the sword of the Spirit which is the Word of God.

When we get home to Heaven our conflict will be over. In Revelation 12 we read of a conflict in Heaven between Michael and his hosts and the dragon and his hosts. But when we go up to Heaven, the mighty foe who throughout the centuries has been the accuser of the people of God, will be cast down to earth. Our conflict is while we are still in this world. I am afraid a great many Christians never realize this. They never stop to think that day by day Satan and his hosts are doing their very best to keep them from honoring the Lord Jesus. He is waging a war to keep Christians from prayer and Bible study so that they will fall and bring shame on the Savior's name. Consequently we see today a largely divided church simply because believers do not know what the real conflict is.

Note that last phrase in verse 12, "Against spiritual wickedness in high places." It seems as though the translators of our beautiful King James version hardly dared accept what this passage really teaches. A clearer translation is, "Against wicked spirits in heavenly places." It is wrong to think that Satan and his hosts are already confined in Hell. Quite the contrary is true; they are still in the heavenly places. That does not mean that they are in the immediate presence of God. Scripture speaks of three heavens: the heaven where the birds fly or the atmosphere, and then the stellar heaven, and beyond all that the Heaven of heavens—the third heaven, the immediate presence of God. Satan and his hosts are represented in Scripture as in the lower heavens. The devil is "the prince of the power of the air." And inasmuch as the eyes of the Lord are everywhere, he is pictured as in the very presence of God as the accuser of the brethren (Revelation 12:10). Our conflict is with these wicked spirits.

We may well sing:

> A charge to keep I have,
> A God to glorify,
> A never-dying soul to save,
> And fit it for the sky.
> Charles Wesley

We have been saved as far as deliverance from the guilt of our sin is concerned, but we are now to be saved practically by conformity to Christ and obedience to the Word of God. In this way we will be prepared in the fullest possible sense for fellowship with Him. May God enable us to be on our guard, to remember that we cannot put the sword out of our hand or rest on past victories as long as we are in this world. "Let him that thinketh he standeth take heed lest he fall" (1 Corinthians 10:12). And yet there is no reason for discouragement because, as our faith and trust are centered in Christ, we may know that "greater is he that is in you, than he that is in the world."

The Whole Armor of God (6:13-17)

As we have considered the Christian's conflict we have found that since it is not with flesh and blood, nor is it with our own carnal nature, we need to be clothed with the whole armor of God. This armor is very different from the garments in which we stand before God through grace. Every one of us who has put our trust in the Lord Jesus Christ has been clothed in the righteousness of God—"He hath clothed me with the garments of salvation, he hath covered me with the robe of righteousness" (Isaiah 61:10). The best robe is His. We stand before God in Christ, but we do not put this robe on ourselves. God has clothed us. But when it comes to the armor for war, we ourselves need to put on each separate piece in order to stand firm in the evil days when the hosts of Hell are attacking our souls and it seems as though we would be defeated. We are not to turn our backs and flee from the foe. We are not to act on the human presumption that "he who fights and runs away may live to fight another day." Rather, we are to face the foe, for there is no armor provided for the back. If we turn our backs and retreat, we expose ourselves to the fiery darts of the wicked one. But as we face the foe unflinchingly in the power of the finished work of Calvary we will be able to stand.

"And having done all, to stand." Where and how do we stand? Is it simply by determination of our own, in some goodness of our own? Not at all. We stand in the perfection of Christ's finished work. The foe cannot harm us there. We meet the enemy in the name of Christ the victor, and we claim the victory because Christ has already defeated him on the cross. There Satan bruised the *heel* of our divine Redeemer, but his own *head* was bruised, and now we are entitled to consider the devil as one already defeated. But, though he knows he is defeated and his doom is sure, he will do everything he can to harass and distress the Christian as long as he is in this world. Therefore we need to stand strong in faith, and resist the devil in the power of the cross of Christ.

"Stand therefore, having your loins girt about with truth." This verse alludes to the long flowing garments worn in many oriental cultures. While perfectly comfortable when worn for leisure, the garments must be drawn about the waist, and held in by a girdle or belt during strenuous movement or conflict so as not to hinder progress. In the same way, you and I as believers are to have our loins girt about with truth. What does this mean? Elsewhere we read, "Gird up the loins of your mind" (1 Peter 1:13). Just as the Oriental's flowing garments were to be tightly fastened that they may not be blown around by the wind, so we are to have our minds surrounded with truth in order that our imaginations may not be "carried about with every wind of doctrine, by the sleight of men, and cunning craftiness, whereby they lie in wait to deceive" (Ephesians 4:14). We are to prepare our minds for action, "bringing into captivity every thought to the obedience of Christ" (2 Corinthians 10:5). In other words, our minds are to be controlled by what God has spoken, not by what we think or hear in the world. Our thoughts are to be brought into subjection to His holy Word.

I wish Christians would come back to the Bible. I am often distressed when people ask me, "What do you think about this, or what do you think about that?" I have to tell them, "It does not make any difference what I think. My thoughts do not amount to anything. The great question is, What has God said? What is written in the Word?" If God's Word does not speak on a particular subject, we have no right to attempt to speak, but where it has given a clear definite declaration, we should be positive and sure in our faith. How important it is that our thoughts are in harmony with God's Word when we have to face the devil. Satan works through wily error, presenting all kinds of false systems and views, and maligning the name of Christ. It is only as our minds are controlled by the Word that we will be able to counter these false teachings. The better you know the Bible, the better fitted you are to meet the assaults of the enemy, and yet some of you have never even read your Bible through once. Perhaps you have never gotten beyond the genealogies. You came right up to them and stopped. You never went any farther. You did not know that hidden in those genealogical chapters there are some of the most beautiful little gems you will find anywhere in the Bible. You will miss them if you are not careful.

A friend of mine used to tell of listening to Andrew Bonar many years ago. Dr. Bonar was speaking on Heaven and the great reunion of loved ones over there. In his eloquent way he pictured the believer newly come from earth walking along the golden street and suddenly meeting a group of Old Testament prophets. In a moment he recognizes them and says, "Why, this is Ezekiel; isn't it?"

"Yes," says Ezekiel, "I am so glad to meet you."

"And this is Micah and Zechariah and Amos."

And then Ezekiel says, "Oh, you know about me, do you? How did you like the book I wrote?"

"Book? What book was that?"

"Oh, surely you remember my book! Did you enjoy it?"

"I am sorry to say I never read it."

And then Micah says, "And what did you think of my book?"

"Let me see; was that in the Old Testament or in the New Testament? It seems to me I remember there was such a book."

Bonar continued, "How would you feel to meet these men when you never have read their books?"

Some of you had better get busy. There is far too much time spent in reading novels and newspapers, and too little time given to the Word of God. Good literature is fine, reading the newspaper is all right, but these things should not crowd out time for reading God's Word. Remember, the Bible is the only Book that will last for all eternity, and anything you can get out of it here you will have for all the ages to come.

The next piece of armor we are to have on is "the breastplate of righteousness." The Bible suggests two types of *righteousness*. The first is that righteousness which is imputed to every believer in the Lord Jesus. It is a glorious truth that we have been made the righteousness of God in Christ (2 Corinthians 5:21). But that is not the righteousness referred to here. You and I do not put on the righteousness of God. God does that for us. But the breastplate of righteousness is something we are to put on. The apostle evidently had in mind Isaiah 59, which refers to a practical righteousness:

> And he saw that there was no man, and wondered that there was no intercessor: therefore his arm brought salvation unto him; and his righteousness, it sustained him. For he put on righteousness as a breastplate, and an helmet of salvation upon

his head; and he put on the garments of vengeance for clothing,
and was clad with zeal as a cloke (Isaiah 59:16-17).

In these verses Isaiah was speaking of the Messiah, our blessed
Lord. He came into this world as a man and was obedient to the will
of God. He put on righteousness as a breastplate, and now you and
I are called to imitate Him by putting on the breastplate of righteousness.

The breastplate covers the heart of the man, and when we think
of the heart we think of the conscience. Unless you as a Christian
keep a good conscience in daily living, you will never be able to
defeat your foe. When the devil comes against you, and you know
there is some hidden, unconfessed sin in your life, you will fall and
will not be able to stand against him. Many a person has failed when
Satan made a tremendous assault on him. People said, "Wasn't it
sad?—such a failure and coming so suddenly." But it was not sud-
den, for there had been an undermining going on weeks and months
and perhaps years—little sins indulged in here and there, unholy
thoughts, wicked things going on that were not dealt with in the
presence of God. Finally, when the enemy attacked in full force
there was an exposed heart because righteousness had not been put
on as the breastplate. If you are witnessing to the unsaved, and they
know that you do not have on the breastplate of righteousness, your
testimony will not amount to very much. You may say to a friend,
"I would like you to come to church with me," and he may say to
you, "I don't know, Jack! It doesn't seem to have done very much
for you." He has been watching you day by day in your work and
has seen that you are just as irritable, impatient, and rude as others,
and he says, "You may talk about good meetings at your church,
but I do not see that they have done much for you." You are not
wearing the breastplate of righteousness. If you want to win in this
battle, you must practice righteousness. Your life must be clean—
there must not be hidden sin, or unholy thinking—if you would
have victory in the conflict. Do not talk about being made the righteousness of God in Christ if you are not living righteously, for when
God justifies a man He makes him just. He justifies us by faith, but
having been justified He now makes us just in our dealings with

other people. That is what is meant by "having on the breastplate of righteousness."

Then, some of us need a new pair of shoes: "And your feet shod with the preparation of the gospel of peace." This means that we are to walk in accordance with the gospel. You tell men that you have been saved by the grace of God, that you have peace with God. Very well, let your life show it. In this metaphor there is also the suggestion of feet swift to carry the gospel of peace. A Spanish translation of this verse is, "Having your feet shod with the joyful readiness to propagate the gospel of peace." But we are not to go about propagating the gospel of peace by word of mouth unless we are living in the power of that gospel message. Otherwise we just bring dishonor on the name of the Lord Jesus Christ.

And then protecting the rest of the armor, "the shield of faith, wherewith ye shall be able to quench all the fiery darts of the wicked." This is the shield of confidence in God. That is what faith is. It is not *the* faith—not *what* you believe, but *how* you believe. It is faith in the sense of confidence and trust—going to meet the enemy with your trust in the living God, not in yourself. For example, a preacher is asked to preach in a gospel meeting. He says to himself, "Well, I have an old sermon here. I have used it 72 times already. It's nearly worn out, but I think it will do for this audience. Yes, I think I will use it again. Years ago when I preached this sermon there were 18 conversions. It must still be good." The devil hears all that, and he says, "I will show you that you have come up against a greater foe than you realize." The meeting is a wretched failure, and the preacher says, "I don't understand it. I have preached that sermon any number of times. I wonder what the trouble was." It was that the confidence of the preacher was in himself and his sermon instead of in the living God. I do not care how many times you have preached on a text, if you ever dare to stand up and preach the Word without getting your message fresh from the living God and going out in confidence in Him instead of in yourself, you will be a failure. I want that lesson to be impressed on my own heart, that is why I am putting it so strongly to you.

The next piece of armor is for our heads: "And take the helmet of salvation." That is, I am to go forth boldly, taking with me the assurance of my salvation through the finished work of Christ. If I have any doubt as to my own salvation, I will have no real confidence when it comes to facing the foe.

The final piece of armor is "the sword of the Spirit, which is the word of God." Do not make a mistake here; the sword of the Spirit is not the Bible. The Bible is the armory, or storehouse of weapons. There are thousands of swords in God's Word and every one of them is powerful and double-edged. There are two different terms in Greek translated "word." There is *logos*, which is the term we usually use, but the other word, *rhema*, is the one used here. It means "a saying"—that is, "And the sword of the Spirit, which is the saying of God." If the devil comes against you and you throw the Bible at him, it is not going to drive him away. You might do that, and go down yourself. But when he comes, and you say, "here is what God says," and you have a definite saying of God to meet the attack, you defeat him.

Take the example of our Lord in the wilderness (Luke 4). The devil came so cunningly and said, "If thou be the Son of God, command that these stones be made bread." Jesus answered, "It is written, that man shall not live by bread alone, but by every word of God." He took the sword out of the armory. You need to know your Bible so that you will be able to meet the devil whenever he comes with such suggestions. Then the devil showed Jesus all the kingdoms of the world, and said, "All this power will I give thee...if thou therefore wilt worship me." Out came another sword and the Lord went at the devil with it. He replied, "It is written, Thou shalt worship the Lord thy God, and him only shalt thou serve." Then the devil tried to use the saying of God himself. He took Jesus up on a pinnacle of the temple and said, "It is written, He shall give his angels charge over thee, to keep thee: And in their hands they shall bear thee up, lest at anytime thou dash thy foot against a stone." Think of the audacity of the devil quoting Scripture, and that to the Lord of life and glory Himself! But he left out a very important part of the verse. In Psalm 91:11-12 we read, "For he shall give his angels charge over thee, to keep thee *in all thy ways*. They shall bear thee up in their hands, lest thou dash thy foot against a stone" (italics added). It was not in Jesus' ordinary *ways* to jump from the temple in order that men would see him carried by angel hands. The Lord countered with another "saying" from the Book of God; He said, "It is said, Thou shalt not tempt the Lord thy God." The sword of the Spirit is the sayings of God. Get to know your Bible, and then when the devil comes against you, you will be able to say, "But the Book says thus and so," and you will have the Word for him. If we want the blessing of God, we must walk in obedience to His Word. We must know our Bible so well that we can draw from this all-sufficient armory the particular saying that we need at a given moment.

Prayer and Supplication in the Holy Spirit (6:18-24)

When you have the various pieces of the armor in place, there is something that must never be omitted. Bunyan speaks of it as actually a part of the armor. He said, "In addition to all the rest there was a piece called 'all prayer'"—"Praying always with all prayer and supplication in the Spirit." The armored believer is independent of the devil because he is utterly dependent on God, and prayer is the source of his dependence. He is to keep the line of communication between himself and his God clear.

During World War I a regiment went into the Argonne Forest and was lost. For days the men were out of touch with headquarters and newspapers wrote of the "lost regiment." When at last they were located, their ranks had been sadly decimated. When a Christian in the conflict with Satan gets out of touch with headquarters, it is a terrible thing. The apostle's admonition is "praying always." The trouble with many of us is that we pray only when we get into difficulty, when times are hard and circumstances are going against us. Then we remember the verse, "Call upon me in the day of trouble: I will deliver thee, and thou shalt glorify me" (Psalm 50:15). But we would be spared a great many of our troubles if, when everything was going well with us, we were just as faithful in prayer as when things were going against us. "Praying always with all prayer."

God declares in His Word that He will not hear the prayer of the wicked. It is an abomination to the Lord. David said, "If I regard iniquity in my heart, the Lord will not hear me." But if I have judged all known sin and am living the life of practical righteousness, I am in that attitude, that position, where I can pray in confidence.

All prayer is an approach to God, but note the added word, *supplication*. This suggests definite petition. It is one thing to approach God in prayer with a heart full of praise and thanksgiving and in a general way commit one's affairs to Him. It is another thing to come with a very definite request for a particular matter or special trouble at a given time. We read:

> Be careful for nothing; but in everything by prayer and supplication [there you have the same word again, it is prayer and petition] with thanksgiving, let your requests be made known unto God. And the peace of God, which passeth all understanding, shall keep your hearts and minds through Christ Jesus (Philippians 4:6-7).

No difficulty that I have to face is too great for God, and nothing that troubles me is too insignificant for His care.

Arthur T. Pierson sat with George Mueller one day, and Mr. Mueller was telling him of some of the wonderful things that God had done for the orphanage at Bristol. As he talked he was writing, and Dr. Pierson noticed that he was having difficulty with his penpoint. Right in the middle of the conversation Mr. Mueller seemed to lose sight of his visitor, he bowed his head for a moment or two in prayer, and then began writing again. Mr. Pierson said, "Mr. Mueller, what were you praying about just now?" "Oh," Mr. Mueller answered, "perhaps you didn't notice that I was having trouble with this penpoint. I haven't another, and this is an important letter, so I was asking the Lord to help me so that I could write it clearly." "Dear me," said Dr. Pierson, "a man who trusts God for millions of pounds also prays about a scratchy penpoint." Yes, you may go to Him about everything.

Notice, we are to make our prayers and petitions "in the Spirit." That admonition should cause many of us to consider the effectiveness of our prayer life. Prayer in the Spirit is prayer in accordance with the mind of the indwelling Holy Spirit of God. No unconverted person, of course, can pray in the Spirit, but there are even Christians who are in such a low carnal condition of soul that it is impossible for them to pray in the Spirit. I cannot pray in the Spirit if I am harboring a grudge against my brother. I cannot pray in the Spirit if there is anyone I will not forgive because of some real or imagined wrong done to me. I cannot pray in the Spirit if I have a selfish motive, or if I am seeking merely my own glory or comfort. I cannot pray in the Spirit if I have a covetous heart.

You remember the apostle James said, "Ye ask, and receive not, because ye ask amiss, that ye may consume it upon your lusts" (James 4:3). I can pray in the Spirit when I am living in the Spirit. Then He, the gracious third person of the Trinity who dwells in every believer, will guide my thoughts as I come to God in prayer. Often, when one is in an unspiritual state, he goes to God requesting certain things. Then when he is restored to fellowship he realizes that he would be better off without them, and so he no longer asks for them. In Psalm 37:4 we read, "Delight thyself also in the Lord; and he shall give thee the desires of thine heart." If I am really delighting myself in the Lord, I will want only those things which will glorify God; I will not be asking from a selfish viewpoint. I will want God to do for me that which will magnify Christ in my life and make Him more precious to my soul.

"Praying always with all prayer and supplication in the Spirit, and watching thereunto with all perseverance." "Watch and pray," our Lord Jesus Christ said, "lest ye enter into temptation," and this, of course, only emphasizes what we have seen already. If I would pray in the Spirit, I must live in the Spirit, and so I am to watch against anything that would come into my life to grieve the Spirit of God and thus hinder real prayer.

As we continue our study of Ephesians 6:18 we note that the Lord would not have me concerned only with my own affairs. He said, "And supplication for all saints." A brother said to me, "For years my interests have largely been in the work in which I myself was engaged, or in connection with certain institutions in which I had a part. But lately I find the Lord is causing me to think of His work everywhere, and of His people in every place." This surely is an evidence of growth in grace. We are so inclined to narrow down our thoughts to our own little circles. We may not pray in the same way as the man who said, "God bless me, and my wife, our son John, and his wife. Us four, and no more," but we do pray most earnestly for those connected intimately with us. We should do this, but in addition let us consider the whole church of God. Let us think of all the people He loves around the world, and hold them up before God's throne in the arms of faith and love. If in this way we go to God, we will never lack subjects about which to speak to Him.

Some years ago I was visiting a very devoted company of Christians in a western State. They had some rather peculiar ideas. They came together weekly to study the Bible and for preaching and observing the Lord's supper, but they had no prayer meeting. I said to them, "Do you never have a prayer meeting?"

A brother said, "Oh no, we have nothing to pray for."

"How is that?" I asked.

"Why, God has blessed us 'with all spiritual blessings in heavenly places in Christ,' so we do not need to pray for spiritual blessings. We do not need to pray for temporal blessings, for we have everything we need. We are well cared for; we have all the land we can farm. We do not need to pray for money, for we have plenty to keep us going. We do not need to pray for wives, for we are all married. We do not need to pray for children; I have thirteen, and Brother so-and-so has fifteen. We have nothing to pray for, so we just give God thanks."

"My dear brother," I said, "I wish, if for nothing else, you would come together to pray for me."

"We can do that at home," he said. "If we came together to pray we wouldn't have anything to say."

"But what about the word, 'And supplication for all saints?' Suppose you do nothing else but come together to remind one another of the Lord's dear children that you know, and spend an hour telling God about them."

But he did not see it. They seemed to have no idea of what prayer really is. Sometime after that I was in Minneapolis. One day I became very sick and was on my back with typhoid fever for six weeks. When at last, a year later, I got out to that western state again, the people of that church said to me, "When we got word that you were so very sick our hearts were greatly burdened and we had two prayer meetings a week to pray for you. But as soon as we got word that you were well enough to go home again, we stopped." "Why did you stop?" I asked. "When flat on my back, I did not have any trouble with the devil. But when I am strong and well, I have to go out to face the foe and I need prayer far more." They looked at me in amazement and said, "We never thought of it in that way."

The apostle Paul himself not only exhorted saints to pray for one another, but he said, "And for me, that utterance may be given unto me, that I may open my mouth boldly" (Ephesians 6:19). I am sure that those of us who stand on public platforms and preach Christ will never know until we get to Heaven how much we owe to the prayers of God's people. It has often come like a benediction when some dear saint, possibly a shut-in, writes to me and says, "My dear brother, daily in prayer I remember you and the work that God has given you to do." How much it means to know that all over this and other lands there are prayer warriors who are crying to God, "Keep that brother from blundering, keep him from sin." There are temptations all around, and how much the man who stands in the pulpit needs divine help that he may be kept from anything that would mar his testimony.

Sometimes God's dear children are far more ready with criticism of preachers than they are with prayer for them. They say, "Well, I don't know; but Mr.— doesn't seem to me to have much power. He doesn't seem to have a gift for making things very clear." And I often feel like saying, "Do you ever pray for him that he may have power, that he may have clarity to so preach the truth that men and women will believe?"

In Acts 14:1 we read that the apostles "so spake, that a great multitude...believed," which implies that one may so speak that no one will believe. What is needed is not only the word of the preacher, but that message backed up by the saints in prayer. It is comforting to know that Christians are praying for you. Paul valued this, and he was the greatest of all the apostles in his ministry. I am sure that at the judgment seat of Christ, when our Lord is rewarding the apostle Paul, He will call up many of the saints of whom we have never heard and have them stand with

Paul, for they were his fellow-workers in his ministry. And He will say, "You held up his hands in prayer, and you must share in the reward."

Paul asked for prayer that he may "make known the mystery of the gospel." This does not mean that the gospel message is something hard to understand, but it is a divine secret that man would never have understood if God Himself had not made it known. One reason why I am absolutely certain that the gospel message is from God is that no man left to himself would ever have dreamed of telling us that God became man to save us from our sins. All human religions take the opposite viewpoint. They try to tell us how man may save himself and eventually obtain a position akin to the Godhead. But not one of them tells us that God became man to save us from our sins. This is the mystery of the gospel, the divine secret that we are called on to proclaim to men.

"I am an ambassador in bonds." What a remarkable declaration! The ambassador from England comes to Washington wearing many medals and decorations. But Paul, the ambassador of the highest court of Heaven says, "Do you want to see my decorations?" And he points to his shackles and says, "I am an ambassador in chains." Somebody has well said, "God is not going to look us over for medals and decorations but for scars, to see what we have endured for Christ's sake." Paul was a suffering, afflicted, jailed ambassador, and he said, "Pray for me, that I may speak boldly, as I ought to speak." And right there in the prison he witnessed for Christ. The very soldiers who were guarding him heard the story of salvation. We read in another of his Epistles, "All the saints salute you, chiefly they that are of Caesar's household." A better translation would be "Caesar's guards" because he is not talking about Caesar's household servants, but of his soldiers. They probably were heathen when sent to guard him, but Christians before they left him. He preached the mystery of the gospel to them and their souls were saved. We will never know how much of the success of Paul's ministry was in answer to prayer until the heavenly records are opened.

In verses 21-22 he wrote the only personal note in the Epistle in which he named anyone else other than himself and the Lord.

But that ye also may know my affairs, and how I do, Tychicus, a beloved brother and faithful minister in the Lord, shall make known to you all things: Whom I have sent unto you for the same purpose, that ye might know our affairs, and that he might comfort your hearts.

In Acts 20:4 we read of Tychicus. He was an Asian. Ephesus was in Asia, and probably Tychicus was well-known to the Ephesian believers, so Paul sent him back in order to give a report as to how things were going with him. Notice the language he used to describe him, "A beloved brother and faithful minister in the Lord." In Colossians 4:7 he wrote, "All my state shall Tychicus declare unto you, who is a beloved brother and a faithful minister and fellowservant in the Lord." Tychicus must have been a very delightful man to meet. It is not often the two things are combined in one man—beloved and faithful. Generally your beloved brother is so gracious and gentle and easy-going that everybody likes him because he does not find fault with anyone. They say, "Isn't he nice?" It is like the lady who, after she had listened to a Scotch preacher, was asked, "What did you think of the sermon? Wasn't it beautiful?" "Yes, it was beautiful," she said; "but it wouldn't hurt a flea." People like the preacher who does not hurt anybody, who draws beautiful word pictures, but never reproves sin. "A good mixer," they call him today. That is the very thing Paul said we were not to be. "Come out from among them, and be ye separate." But as a rule they are the loved kind of preachers. On the other hand, the faithful brother is apt to be so rigid that he gets a little legalistic and goes around clubbing people with the Word, and saying, "I don't care what people think of me; I am going to be faithful." He is rather disagreeable and no one likes to get too close to men like that. But Tychicus combined in himself the beloved pastor and the faithful exhorter. That is a wonderful combination, too high for most of us to attain.

And then in verses 23-24 we have the closing words of Paul's letter. You will observe there are no personal salutations in Ephesians. The reason probably was that the Epistle to the Ephesians was a circular letter, intended not only for the saints in Ephesus, but sent around a circle of assemblies until it reached Laodicea. Paul, writing to the Colossians, said, "Read the epistle from Laodicea." Some think this is a reference to a lost letter, but it is undoubtedly this letter to the Ephesians. And on account of its general character there are no personal salutations for individuals in the Ephesian church.

"Peace be to the brethren, and love with faith, from God the Father and the Lord Jesus Christ." Paul prayed that the Ephesians would receive the peace which is given to all who have learned to commit everything to the care of our Savior. Then he coupled love for the saints with faith in the Lord Jesus Christ, which is the gift of God the Father through His Son.

He closed with the characteristic Pauline salutation, "Grace be with all them that love our Lord Jesus Christ." And then he added a penetrating phrase at the very end, "in sincerity," or as other translations say, "in incorruptness." In other words, those who love our Lord Jesus Christ will exhibit their love by holy living. This is how we show in a practical way that we are one with Him in the heavenly places.

AUTHOR BIOGRAPHY

HENRY ALLAN IRONSIDE, one of this century's greatest preachers, was born in Toronto, Canada, on October 14, 1876. He lived his life by faith; his needs at crucial moments were met in the most remarkable ways.

Though his classes stopped with grammar school, his fondness for reading and an incredibly retentive memory put learning to use. His scholarship was well recognized in academic circles with Wheaton College awarding an honorary Litt.D. in 1930 and Bob Jones University an honorary D.D. in 1942. Dr. Ironside was also appointed to the boards of numerous Bible institutes, seminaries, and Christian organizations.

"HAI" lived to preach and he did so widely throughout the United States and abroad. E. Schuyler English, in his biography of Ironside, revealed that during 1948, the year HAI was 72, and in spite of failing eyesight, he "gave 569 addresses, besides participating in many other ways." In his eighteen years at Chicago's Moody Memorial Church, his only pastorate, every Sunday but two had at least one profession of faith in Christ.

H. A. Ironside went to be with the Lord on January 15, 1951. Throughout his ministry, he authored expositions on 51 books of the Bible and through the great clarity of his messages led hundreds of thousands, worldwide, to a knowledge of God's Word. His words are as fresh and meaningful today as when first preached.

The official biography of Dr. Ironside, *H. A. Ironside: Ordained of the Lord*, is available from the publisher.

THE WRITTEN MINISTRY OF
H. A. IRONSIDE

Expositions

Joshua	Acts
Ezra	Romans
Nehemiah	1 & 2 Corinthians
Esther	Galatians
Psalms (1-41 only)	Ephesians
Proverbs	Philippians
Song of Solomon	Colossians
Isaiah	1 & 2 Thessalonians
Jeremiah	1 & 2 Timothy
Lamentations	Titus
Ezekiel	Philemon
Daniel	Hebrews
The Minor Prophets	James
Matthew	1 & 2 Peter
Mark	1,2, & 3 John
Luke	Jude
John	Revelation

Doctrinal Works

Baptism	Letters to a Roman Catholic
Death and Afterward	Priest
Eternal Security of the Believer	The Levitical Offerings
Holiness: The False and	Not Wrath But Rapture
the True	Wrongly Dividing the Word
The Holy Trinity	of Truth

Historical Works

The Four Hundred Silent Years
A Historical Sketch of the Brethren Movement

Other works by the author are brought back into print from time to time. All of this material is available from your local Christian bookstore or from the publisher.

LOIZEAUX

A Heritage of Ministry...

Paul and Timothy Loizeaux began their printing and publishing activities in the farming community of Vinton, Iowa, in 1876. Their tools were rudimentary: a hand press, several fonts of loose type, ink, and a small supply of paper. There was certainly no dream of a thriving commercial enterprise. It was merely the means of supplying the literature needs for their own ministries, with the hope that the Lord would grant a wider circulation. It wasn't a business; it was a ministry.

Our Foundation Is the Word of God

We stand without embarrassment on the great fundamentals of the faith: the inspiration and authority of Scripture, the deity and spotless humanity of our Lord Jesus Christ, His atoning sacrifice and resurrection, the indwelling of the Holy Spirit, the unity of the church, the second coming of the Lord, and the eternal destinies of the saved and lost.

Our Mission Is to Help People Understand God's Word

We are not in the entertainment business. We only publish books and computer software we believe will be of genuine help to God's people, both through the faithful exposition of Scripture and practical application of its principles to contemporary need.

Faithfulness to the Word and consistency in what we publish have been hallmarks of Loizeaux through four generations. And that means when you see the name Loizeaux on the outside, you can trust what is on the inside. That is our promise to the Lord...and to you.

If Paul and Timothy were to visit us today they would still recognize the work they began in 1876. Because some very important things haven't changed at all...this is still a ministry.